Using Film

to Visualize Principles and Practices

Joseph E. Champoux

The Robert O. Anderson Schools of Management
The University of New Mexico

South-Western College Publishing
Thomson Learning™

Australia • Canada • Mexico • Singapore • Spain • United Kingdom • United States

Management: Using Film to Visualize Principles and Practices, First Edition, by Joseph E. Champoux

PUBLISHER	Jack Calhoun
EXECUTIVE EDITOR	John Szilagyi
DEVELOPMENTAL EDITOR	Judith O'Neill
MARKETING MANAGER	Rob Bloom
MEDIA AND TECHNOLOGY EDITOR	Kurt Gerdenich
MEDIA PRODUCTION EDITOR	Kristen Meere
EDITORIAL PRODUCTION AND INTERNAL DESIGN	James Reidel, Logatorial Editorial Services
COVER DESIGN	Michael H. Stratton
PHOTOGRAPHY MANAGER	Cary Benbow
MANUFACTURING COORDINATOR	Sandee Milewski
PRINTER	Westgroup

ISBN 0-324-05359-2

Printed in the United States of America
1 2 3 4 5 03 02 01 00

For more information contact South-Western College Publishing, 5101 Madison Road, Cincinnati, Ohio, 45227 or find us on the Internet at http://www.swcollege.com

For permission to use material from this text or product, contact us by
• telephone: 1-800-730-2214
• fax: 1-800-730-2215
• web: http://www.thomsonrights.com

This book is printed on acid-free paper.

To Jean-Marc and Jean-André, in honor of the men you have become

C o n t e n t s

Introduction to Organizations and Management

An **organization** is a system of two or more persons, engaged in cooperative action, trying to reach some purpose (Barnard 1938, 73). Organizations are bounded systems of structured social interaction featuring authority relations, communication systems, and the use of incentives. Examples of organizations include businesses, hospitals, colleges, retail stores, and prisons (Blau and Scott 1962; Etzioni 1964; Scott 1964).

We are all part of organizations, whether we want to be or not. You are now part of an organization—your college or university. In your daily round of activities, you move from one organization to another. You may shop at a store, deal with a government agency, or go to work. Understanding organizations and their management can give you significant insights into systems that have major effects on you.

The scenes discussed in this chapter come from the following films:

- Antz
- Brazil
- Catch 22
- The Secret of My Success

Antz offers an animated symbolic rendering of the world of work. *Brazil* offers a comic, satiric look at bureaucracies. *Catch 22* describes the now famous "catch," which shows that managers build policies into their organizations with little prior knowledge of their effects. *The Secret of My Success* shows the first-day-at-work experiences of a newly hired college graduate.

Antz

Color, 1998
Running time: 1 hour, 23 minutes
Rating: PG
Distributed by *DreamWorks Home Entertainment*

Z (played by Woody Allen) is an insignificant worker ant in a massive ant colony. He is trying to find his role in life and pursue Princess Bala (Sharon Stone). Everything changes after he trades places with his soldier ant friend Weaver (Sylvester Stallone). A termite war and the pursuit of the evil General Mandible (Gene Hackman) transport Z's life to new and unexpected places. This Dream-Works production is a wonderful example of modern computer animation.*

Scenes (Start: 0:04:11 — Stop: 0:11:21 — 7 minutes)

These scenes start after the opening credits with a shot of the New York skyline. Z says in the voice-over, "All my life I've lived and worked in the big city." They end as General Mandible and Colonel Cutter (Christopher Walken) leave to meet the queen. Mandible says, "Our very next stop, Cutter."

What to Watch for and Ask Yourself

- What are the major work-related issues raised in these scenes?
- Do you see these issues in your work experiences?
- What is your preferred "world of work?"

---

*Originally suggested by Greg McNeil, one of my students at The Robert O. Anderson School of Management, The University of New Mexico. — J.E.C.

Concepts or Examples

 Personal needs

 Meaningful work

Supervisory behavior

Worker contribution to the larger organization

Analysis

_____

_____

_____

_____

_____

_____

Personal Reactions

_____

_____

_____

_____

_____

Brazil

Color, 1985
Running Time: 2 hours, 11 minutes
Rating: R
Distributor: *MCA Home Video*

This film is a surrealistic, comedic look at a future world dominated by massive bureaucracies. Directed by former Monty Python member Terry Gilliam, the film follows bureaucrat Sam Lowry (Jonathan Price) in his search for the mysterious Jill Layton (Kim Greist). The engaging photography helps show the oppressiveness of bureaucracy in this future society.

Scenes

Two sets of scenes introduce you to the Ministry of Information and show how it functions. They each show different aspects of organizational behavior.

1. Start: 0:01:08 — Stop: 0:10:24 — 9 minutes

The first scenes start at the beginning of the film with the shot of clouds and the song *Brazil* in the background. They end after Mr. Kurtzman (Ian Holm) asks whether anyone has seen Sam Lowry.

2. Start: 0:12:54 — Stop: 0:16:06 — 3 minutes

The second set of scenes, which follow the scenes of Sam Lowry preparing to go to work, start with a view of the Ministry of Information's giant icon They end after Jill Layton pushes the surveillance machine out of her way and storms out of the Ministry.

What to Watch for and Ask Yourself

- What type of organizational behavior do these scenes show?
- Are there any manifest functions to this behavior?
- Are there any latent dysfunctions to the same behavior?

Concepts or Examples

☐ Organization

☐ Organizational behavior

☐ Bureaucracy

☐ Bureausis (i.e., intolerance of bureaucratic behavior)

☐ Bureaucratic behavior

☐ Bureaupathology (i.e., excessive bureaucratic behavior)

☐ Means–ends inversion

Analysis

_____

_____

_____

_____

_____

_____

Personal Reactions

_____

_____

_____

_____

_____

Catch 22

Color, 1970
Running Time: 2 hours, 1 minute
Rating: R
Distributor: *Paramount Home Video*

Army Air Force officers are bone weary from flying too many missions during World War II. This black comedy satire pokes fun at military life and shows the stress of war. Captain Yossarian (Alan Arkin) makes endless efforts to not fly any more missions.

Scene (Start: 0:09:32 — Stop: 0:11:52 — 3 minutes)

This scene starts with the shot of Doc Daneeka's face (Jack Guilford) as he says, "There's nothing wrong with it." Yossarian replies, "Well look at it once." It follows the dining hall discussion about Yossarian's feelings of persecution. The scene ends as Doc appears upside down and says, "It's the best there is." The film then cuts to Major Danby (Richard Benjamin) talking to the flight crews about the day's mission.

What to Watch for and Ask Yourself

- Are there examples of excessively bureaucratic behavior in this scene?
- If so, what specific behaviors do you see?
- Have you had any experiences similar to those shown in the scene?

Concepts or Examples

☐ Bureaucratic behavior

☐ Bureaupathology (i.e., excessive bureaucratic behavior)

☐ Rules, policies, procedures

☐ Means–ends inversion

Analysis

_____

_____

_____

_____

_____

Personal Reactions

_____

_____

_____

_____

_____

The Secret of My Success (I)

Color, 1987
Running Time: 1 hour, 50 minutes
Rating: PG-13
Distributor: *MCA Home Video*

This film is an entertaining look at corporate life featuring power, negotiation, and sexual shenanigans. It begins when college graduate Brantley Foster (Michael J. Fox) leaves his Kansas home and goes to New York. He wants to succeed as an executive but can only land a job in the mailroom. By impersonating an executive, and frantically balancing his mailroom and executive jobs, he hopes to impress the beautiful Christy Wills (Helen Slater). Another scene is discussed on page 106.

Scene (Start: 0:18:54 — Stop: 0:22:01 — 3 minutes)

The scene starts with a shot of the mailroom and Brantley Foster arriving for his first workday. It ends after the lunch conversation on the street with coworker Fred Melrose (John Pankow). The movie then cuts to Brantley talking to a Research Department clerk (Mary Catherine Wright).

What to Watch for and Ask Yourself

- What do these scenes suggest you will learn on your first day on the job?
- From whom did Brantley learn the key features of his job?
- Was there any evidence of clear status relationships in this company?

Concepts or Examples

- ☐ Required work behavior
- ☐ Jargon
- ☐ Social relationships
- ☐ Social status
- ☐ Status relationships

Analysis

_____

_____

_____

_____

_____

_____

Personal Reactions

_____

_____

_____

_____

_____

References

Barnard, C. I. 1938. *The Functions of the Executive*. Cambridge: Harvard University Press.

Blau, P. M., and W. R. Scott. 1962. *Formal Organizations*. San Francisco: Chandler Publishing Co.

Etzioni, A. 1964. *Modern Organizations*. Englewood Cliffs, NJ: Prentice Hall.

Scott, W. R. 1964. Theory of Organizations. In *Handbook of Modern Sociology*, ed. R. E. L. Faris. Chicago: Rand McNally, 485–529.

CHAPTER 2

Workforce Diversity

Workforce diversity refers to variations in workforce composition based on personal and background factors of employees—or potential employees. Those factors include age, gender, race, ethnicity, physical ability, and sexual orientation. Other factors focus on family status, such as a single parent, a dual-career relationship, or a person with responsibilities for aging parents (Hayles & Russell 1997; Jackson & Assocs.1992; Jamieson and O'Mara 1991).

Bureau of Labor Statistics' (BLS) projections (Fullerton 1997) show the next century's workforce as having more female and minority workers. Age diversity will also continue with 15 percent of the labor force at age 55 or over in 2006. The expected gender and ethnic profile of the labor force in the year 2006 shows 47 percent women and 29 percent minority workers.

People from different social backgrounds, cultures, and language groups bring different worldviews to an organization (Bond and Pyle 1998). They view issues and problems at work through different perceptual lenses. If properly managed, these different views present opportunities to organizations, but they also increase the potential for conflict.

The scenes discussed in this chapter show aspects of diversity and come from the following films:

- Babe
- Brassed Off!
- James and the Giant Peach
- Young Frankenstein

The scenes from *Babe* show how hard it is for a person (in this case, a young pig) to change basic characteristics. *Brassed Off!*, a British film, shows the grudging acceptance of a female into an all-male brass band. *James and the Giant Peach* is an eye-popping, stop-motion animated film with a striking diversity scene. *Young Frankenstein* is a delightful portrayal of the acceptance of differences in the famous blind hermit scene with Gene Hackman and Peter Boyle.

Babe

Color, 1995
Running Time: 1 hour, 32 minutes
Rating: G
Distributor: *Universal Studios Home Video*

A charming Australian film featuring an eccentric, quiet farmer who trains a pig he won at the fair to herd his sheep. His eccentricity turns to determination when he enters the pig in the Australian National Sheepdog Championships. The Academy Award-winning visual effects include a seamless mixture of animatronic doubles, computer images, and live animals (Champoux 1999).

Scenes

There are two sets of scenes that show diversity, dimensions of diversity, and diversity and performance. One set is early in the film; the other set ends the film.

1. (Start: 0:44:10 — Stop: 0:50:25 — 6 minutes)

The scenes start with Farmer Hoggett (James Cromwell) opening his new motor-powered gate and calling his dogs. Hoggett says, "Come Rex. Come Fly. Come Pig." The scenes end as a horse-drawn wagon goes down a hill. Babe (Christine Cavanaugh) and Fly (Miriam Margolyes) are talking. Fly says to Babe, "No, no, now. I think you better leave that to me." The sheep call the dogs "wolves."

2. (Start: 1:24:44 — Stop: 1:32:29 — 7 minutes)

These scenes start as the Committee meeting room door opens. The Chairman of the Judges (Marshall Napier) tells Farmer Hoggett that there is no rule to block his entry of Babe in the Australian National Sheep Dog trials. The scenes end after Babe gets his score and Hoggett says, "That'll do pig. That'll do." A circle closes on Babe and the screen goes black.

What to Watch for and Ask Yourself

- Are Babe's methods of herding sheep different from those used by sheepdogs? If you answer yes, what are the differences?
- Does Babe discover that he cannot successfully herd sheep as a sheep dog herds them? What does he do?
- Does Farmer Hoggett accept Babe for what he is—a pig not a sheep dog?

Concepts or Examples

☐ Diversity

☐ Different routes to the same goal

☐ Cannot change who you are

☐ Valuing diversity

☐ Increased conflict potential

☐ Diversity and performance

Analysis

_____

_____

_____

_____

_____

Personal Reactions

_____

_____

_____

_____

_____

Brassed Off!

Color, 1996
Running Time: 1 hour, 41 minutes
Rating: R
Distributor: *Miramax Home Entertainment*

A touching story about the economic woes of the fictional coalmining town of Grimly, Yorkshire, England. The town faces the closing of its mine, a major source of employment. Playing in the mine's brass band is the only source of hope for many workers. Gloria Mullins (Tara Fitzgerald) arrives and becomes the band's first female player. Charming performances and great music soften the sadness of the story. The Grimethorpe Colliery Band plays the brass band music. *Brassed off* is British slang for dejected or upset (Champoux 1999).

Scenes (Start: 0:20:57 — Stop: 0:32:08 — 11 minutes)

The scenes follow the shots of Danny (Pete Postlethwaite) and his son riding Danny's bike to the rehearsal site. They open with a close-up shot of the band's euphonium section. This scene sequence includes intercut scenes of union-management negotiations at the mine's office. The scenes end after Gloria says, "If I'm allowed." Danny says, "Don't be soft [silly], lass. You were born here." The screen goes black and the movie cuts to a neighborhood scene.

What to Watch for and Ask Yourself

- Do the band members openly accept Gloria from the beginning?
- What persuades them that she can be an acceptable member?
- Do you expect that her presence will help the band in its later competition?

Concepts or Examples

☐ Workforce diversity   ☐ Heterogeneous group

☐ Gender-based diversity   ☐ Performance

☐ Homogeneous group

Analysis

_____

_____

_____

_____

_____

Personal Reactions

_____

_____

_____

_____

_____

James and the Giant Peach (I)

Color, 1996
Running Time: 1 hour, 20 minutes
Rating: G
Distributor: *Walt Disney Home Video*

This captivating stop-motion animated film directed by Tim Burton follows a young boy's quest to leave his awful aunts and go to New York City. He discovers a giant peach on a tree in his yard. James (Paul Terry) enters it and becomes part of the diverse world of Grasshopper (Simon Callow), Centipede (Richard Dreyfuss), Ladybug (Jane Reeves), Glowworm (Miriam Margolyes), Spider (Susan Sarandon), and Earthworm (David Thewlis). This film is brilliantly animated with a captivating though bizarre story. Another scene from *James and the Giant Peach* is discussed on page 76.

Scene (Start: 0:26:07 — Stop: 0:31:19 — 5 minutes)

This sequence starts with the peach opening and emitting green light. James climbs in and meets its occupants. They all sing "That's the Life for Me." The sequence ends after Centipede climbs the ladder.

What to Watch for and Ask Yourself

- What dimensions of diversity appear in this scene?
- What would you predict for this group working together?
- Would you expect conflict within the group because of their extreme diversity?

Concepts or Examples

☐ Workforce diversity

☐ Heterogeneous group

☐ Homogeneous group

☐ Group performance

☐ Intra-group conflict

☐ Dimensions of diversity

Analysis

_____

_____

_____

_____

_____

_____

Personal Reactions

_____

_____

_____

_____

_____

Young Frankenstein

Black and White, 1974
Running Time: 1 hour, 42 minutes
Rating: PG-13
Distributor: *20th Century Fox Home Entertainment*

Young Dr. Frederick Frankenstein (Gene Wilder) works in his grandfather's laboratory with the help of loony assistant Igor (Marty Feldman). This hilarious film spoofs the 1930s Frankenstein movies. Dr. Frankenstein succeeds in creating a daffy Monster (Peter Boyle) who seeks acceptance and affection but has a hard time finding it. Director Mel Brooks used the original laboratory props from the 1931 *Frankenstein* to make this film. (Champoux 1999)

Scene (Start: 1:08:39 — Stop: 1:13:19 — 5 minutes)

The camera zooms to a house and goes to candles on a table. Blind Hermit (Gene Hackman) is praying. The scene ends after Monster leaves with his finger on fire. Blind Hermit says, "Wait! Wait! Where are you going? I was going to make espresso." The screen goes black.

What to Watch for and Ask Yourself

- Does this scene show the open acceptance of people's differences?
- What are the functional and dysfunctional results of such acceptance?
- Is there any evidence of stereotyping in this scene?

Concepts or Examples

☐ Perception
☐ Diversity
☐ Acceptance of differences

☐ Stereotyping
☐ Dimensions of diversity
☐ Valuing diversity

Analysis

_____

_____

_____

_____

_____

Personal Reactions

_____

_____

_____

_____

_____

References

Bond, M. A., and J. L. Pyle. 1998. The Ecology of Diversity in Organizational Settings: Lessons from a Case Study. *Human Relations* 51: 589–623.

Champoux, J. E. 1999. Seeing and Valuing Diversity in Film. *Educational Media International* 36: 310–316. *Note:* Portions of this article have been used in this chapter with permission.

Fullerton, Jr., H. N. 1997. Labor Force 2006: Slowing Down and Changing Composition. *Monthly Labor Review* 120: 23–38.

Hayles, V. R., and A. M. Russell. 1997. *The Diversity Directive: Why Some Initiatives Fail & What to Do About It*. Chicago: Irwin Professional Publishing.

Jackson, S. E. and Associates, eds. 1992. *Diversity in the Workplace: Human Resources Initiatives*. New York: Guilford Press.

Jamieson, D., and J. O'Mara. 1991. *Managing Workforce 2000: Gaining the Diversity Advantage*. San Francisco: Jossey-Bass.

CHAPTER 3

Quality Management

major thrust of American management is the quality of products and services (Champoux 1999). Although quality management can be traced to the 1920s (Radford 1922), American organizations did not embrace it until the early 1980s (Garvin 1988; Gehani 1993). Quality management has many names including Total Quality Control, Total Quality Management, Total Quality Leadership, Leadership Through Quality, Market Driven Quality, and Continuous Process Improvement. **Quality Management** (QM) is a philosophy and system of management that includes tools and techniques that help organizations manage for quality in services, products, and processes. Although its roots are in manufacturing, QM is a management system that can bring major improvements to any organization.

QM emphasizes a long-term commitment to continuous quality improvement. It stresses that quality is everyone's job, not the job of a quality-control department. QM is intensely customer focused and demands that all members of the organization share that focus (Legnick-Hall 1996). QM emphasizes high involvement in the work process. It also emphasizes communication in all directions: top-down, bottom-up, and laterally. This feature follows directly from the requirements of cooperation and high involvement.

Scenes from these four films help show the customer focus aspect of QM:

- Five Easy Pieces
- The Hospital
- Breakfast at Tiffany's
- Never Give a Sucker an Even Break

Jack Nicholson's classic chicken salad sandwich scene in *Five Easy Pieces* shows the meaning of no customer service. The scene from *The Hospital* shows an insensitive insurance clerk's behavior. An opposite scene appears in *Breakfast at Tiffany's*, in which a Tiffany's clerk tries to satisfy Holly Golightly's desire to stay within her budget. W. C. Fields plays an irritable restaurant customer in *Never Give a Sucker an Even Break*.

Five Easy Pieces

Color, 1970
Running Time: 1 hour, 38 minutes
Rating: R
Distributor: *Columbia Tristar Home Video*

A young Jack Nicholson richly portrays Robert Eroica Dupea, a musician who gave up his career to work in the oil fields. He is trying to return home to pay his last wishes to his dying father. Along the way, he picks up some female hitch-hikers who each are character studies. They stop at a roadside restaurant for food where the famous chicken salad sandwich scene unfolds.

Scene (Start: 0:45:42 — Stop: 0:47:33 — 2 minutes)

This scene starts as Dupea begins to order his food from the waitress. He says, "I'd like a, ah, a plain omelet. No potatoes, tomatoes instead." It ends with the group riding in the car and Palm Apodaca (Helena Kallianiotes) saying, "No, but it was very clever. I would have just punched her out."

What to Watch for and Ask Yourself

- What does this scene show about customer service?
- Was Robert Dupea an unreasonable customer?
- Was the waitress flexible or inflexible in her customer focus?

Concepts or Examples

- ☐ Customer service
- ☐ Quality management
- ☐ Customer focus
- ☐ Flexible policies
- ☐ Inflexible policies

Analysis

_____

_____

_____

_____

_____

Personal Reactions

_____

_____

_____

_____

_____

The Hospital

Color, 1971
Running Time: 1 hour, 42 minutes
Rating: PG
Distributor: *MGM/UA Home Video*

A caustic, satirical look at the workings of a big city hospital. This film, which won Paddy Chayefsky an Oscar for best screenplay in 1971, features many compelling scenes of relationships among a hospital's staff and patients. The selected scene is a highpoint in this film's unrelenting black comedy.

Scene (Start: 0:23:15 — Stop: 0:26:38 — 3 minutes)

The scene starts in the emergency room with Sally (Frances Sternhagen) from accounting asking for Mr. Henning. She also asks other patients in the area about their health insurance. The scene ends after Dr. Spezio (Rehn Scofield) says the patient in the holding area is dead.

What to Watch for and Ask Yourself

- Does the scene show the presence or absence of a customer focus?
- Would a customer focus view of Sally's role in accounting better serve the hospital? Why or why not?
- What other unintended dysfunctions does this scene show?

Concepts or Examples

☐ Customer focus

☐ Managing for quality

☐ Excessive bureaucratic focus

☐ Customer needs or desires

☐ Bureaucracy

Analysis

_____

_____

_____

_____

_____

_____

Personal Reactions

_____

_____

_____

_____

_____

Breakfast at Tiffany's

Color, 1961
Running Time: 1 hour, 55 minutes
Rating: NR
Distributor: *Paramount Home Video*

An endearing Truman Capote story about Holly Golightly (Audrey Hepburn), a young rural woman who becomes a New York playgirl.* She has a shaky romance with writer Paul Varjak (George Peppard). Though now almost a period film of mid-century New York life, the comedy and charming romance come through for any audience. The film features Henry Mancini's Academy Award winning song, "Moon River."

Scene (Start: 1:08:40 — Stop: 1:13:16 — 4 minutes)

This scene starts with Jack and Holly walking along a Manhattan street. They follow the scene of Jack opening champagne in Holly's apartment. It ends after Holly kisses the Tiffany's clerk (John MacGiver) and says, "Didn't I tell you this is a lovely place."

What to Watch for and Ask Yourself

- Was the clerk trying to focus on the needs and desires of Jack and Holly?
- What did he do to meet their budget requirements?
- Would you expect this type of customer service in a modern, upscale jewelry store?

---

* Originally suggested by Elizabeth McCormick, Olivia Timmons, and Jeff Loafman, my students at The Robert O. Anderson School of Management, The University of New Mexico. — J.E.C.

Concepts or Examples

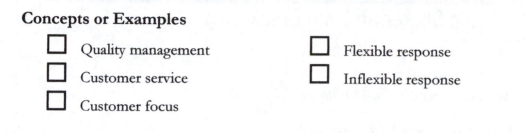

☐ Quality management   ☐ Flexible response

☐ Customer service   ☐ Inflexible response

☐ Customer focus

Analysis

_____

_____

_____

_____

_____

Personal Reactions

_____

_____

_____

_____

_____

Never Give a Sucker an Even Break

Black and White, 1941
Running Time: 1 hour, 11 minutes
Rating: NR
Distributor: *Kartes Video Communications*

The legendary comedian W. C. Fields—in his last starring role—plays himself in this film that is filled with many funny scenes and no real plot. In addition to Fields' classic slapstick, the final car chase scene is a near classic in this film genre.

Scene (Start: 0:05:19 — Stop: 0:07:39 — 3 minutes)

This scene starts with a fade-in shot of the front of a restaurant and W. C. Fields entering. It ends with Fields muttering, "These flies get the best of everything. Go away. Go away Go away . . ." The film then cuts to Sound Stage 6 and a young woman singing.

What to Watch for and Ask Yourself

- Does the waitress show a concern for her customers?
- Is Fields simply a cranky customer who did not deserve careful service?
- What would you do in this situation, assuming you took it seriously?

Concepts or Examples

☐ Customer focus   ☐ Customer satisfaction

☐ Meeting customer needs ☐ Customer behavior

Analysis

_____

_____

_____

_____

_____

Personal Reactions

_____

_____

_____

_____

_____

References

Champoux, J. E. 1999. Management Context of Not-for-Profit Organizations in the Next Millennium: Diversity, Quality, Technology, Global Environment, and Ethics. In *The Nonprofit Management Handbook*. 2d ed. 1999 supplement. Edited by T. D. Connors. New York: John Wiley & Sons, 7–9. *Note:* Parts of the introduction for this chapter have been adapted from this essay.

Garvin, D. A. 1988. *Managing Quality: The Strategic and Competitive Edge*. New York: Free Press.

Gehani, R. R. 1993. Quality Value-Chain: A Meta-Synthesis of Frontiers of Quality Movement. *Academy of Management Executive* 7: 29-42.

Information Week. 1993. A Cure for IBM's Blues? Retiring Exec Prescribes a Continuing Focus on Quality. *Information Week* (January 4): 48-49.

Lengnick-Hall, C. A. 1996. Customer Contributions to Quality: A Different View of the Customer-Oriented Firm. *Academy of Management Review* 21: 791–824.

Radford, G. S. 1922. *The Control of Quality in Manufacturing*. New York: Ronald Press.

Technology

Changes in computing power, features, and telecommunications continue to revolutionize what organizations will do in the future. High-speed processors larger memory capacity, and broadband Internet connections have made desktop PCs even more powerful business tools in the age of e-commerce. Laptops and palmtops permit connection to the Internet using ports in airport telephones, aircraft telephones, or cybercafés. Tracking appointments and staying connected continues to get easier. Email, voicemail, videoconferencing, and teleconferencing are widely used and will increase in use in the future (Caincross 1998; Quain 1998).

A revolution in materials technology is unfolding. Some materials already in use are carbon fiber composites and optical fibers, the basis of tennis rackets and communication cable respectively. Others, such as superpolymers, amorphous metal alloys, and superconductors, add to a growing list of human-created materials. Innovations in product ideas and technological solutions no longer depend on naturally existing materials (Gross and Port 1998).

This chapter discusses films that show different **technologies** and their effects on behavior and organizations. These films include:

- The Net
- The Saint
- My Best Friend's Wedding
- You've Got Mail

An early scene from *The Net* shows the effects of the Internet on people's behavior. *The Saint* has a scene centered on fusion technology that shows how technology can affect power relationships in organizations. *My Best Friend's Wedding* has a closing scene that shows technology-induced social interaction. *You've Got Mail* is about an interpersonal relationship—conducted over the Internet and face-to-face.

The Net

Color, 1995
Running Time: 1 hour, 54 minutes
Rating: PG-13
Distributor: *Columbia Tristar Home Video*

Mousy computer systems analyst Angela Bennett (Sandra Bullock) discovers an Internet program that easily accesses classified databases. Others know what she has discovered and set out to eliminate her identity from various official records. Then they try to kill her.

Scenes (Start: 0:10:11 — Stop: 0:15:47 — 6 minutes)

The sequence starts with a panning shot of the sky and over a neighborhood. The camera zooms to Angela typing at her computer. It ends after Angela says, "Yeh, I know." She turns off her computer. The movie cuts to her mother playing piano.

What to Watch for and Ask Yourself

- What technological effects on social interaction do these scenes show?
- Which technologies do these scenes show?
- Is this an example of modern telecommuting—working from home or being part of a virtual team?

Concepts or Examples

☐ Various technologies

☐ Effects of technology on social interaction

☐ Virtual team

☐ Telecommuting

Analysis

_____

_____

_____

_____

_____

Personal Reactions

_____

_____

_____

_____

_____

The Saint

Color, 1997
Running Time: 1 hour, 56 minutes
Rating: PG-13
Distributor: *Paramount Home Video*

Russian strong man Ivan Tretiak (Rade Serbedzija) hires super thief and master of disguises Simon Templar (Val Kilmer) to steal a fusion formula from a beautiful scientist. Templar falls in love with Dr. Emma Russell (Eilzabeth Shue). He double-crosses Tretiak, setting in motion a series of action scenes in which Templer and Russell escape from danger. The film has many wonderful location shots of Oxford University and Moscow.

Scene (Start: 1:48:56 — Stop: 1:52:09 — 3 minutes)

The scene starts as Ilya Tretiak (Valery Nikolaev) puts a microphone on Ivan Tretiak. They end after the fusion experiment works and an aerial shot of Moscow. A voice over says, "And he made no threat to contact you in the future"? The movie cuts to Scotland Yard detectives interviewing Dr. Emma Russell. These scenes include shots of Simon Templar and President Karpov (Eugene Lazarev).

What to Watch for and Ask Yourself

- Did Ivan Tretiak believe he had the power to overthrow President Karpov?
- Did the fusion technology change the people's perception of Tretiak's and Karpov's power?
- Can technology have such effects in real organizations?

Concepts or Examples

- ☐ Technology
- ☐ Power
- ☐ Power relationships
- ☐ Perceptions of power

Analysis

_____

_____

_____

_____

_____

_____

Personal Reactions

_____

_____

_____

_____

_____

_____

My Best Friend's Wedding (I)

Color, 1997
Running Time: 1 hour, 45 minutes
Rating: PG-13
Distributor: *Columbia TriStar Home Video*

Michael O'Neal (Dermot Mulroney) a sportswriter and restaurant critic Julianne Potter (Julia Roberts) are best friends. They have agreed to marry each other if neither has found a partner by age 28. Michael falls for the wealthy and beautiful Kimmy (Cameron Diaz). Julianne now realizes she loves Michael and tries to stop the wedding. Her bungled efforts add great humor to the film. Beautifully photographed on location in Chicago. A scene from *My Best Friend's Wedding* is also discussed on page 86.

Scene (Start: 1:46:09 — Stop: 1:49:49 — 4 minutes)

The scene starts with Michael and Kimmy driving away. The film cuts to a close-up shot of Julianne watching them go. It ends with George (Rupert Everett) and Julianne dancing. The screen goes black and the film cuts to the closing credits.

What to Watch for and Ask Yourself

- Did technology affect social interaction in this scene?
- George is a homosexual; Julianne is a heterosexual. Do these differences keep them apart?
- Could you expect technology to have similar affects in real organizations?

Concepts or Examples

☐ Technology ☐ Attraction as lovers

☐ Social interaction ☐ Cellular telephones

☐ Attraction as friends

Analysis

_____

_____

_____

_____

_____

_____

Personal Reactions

_____

_____

_____

_____

_____

You've Got Mail

Color, 1998
Running Time: 2 hours
Rating: PG
Distributor: *Warner Home Video*

Neighborhood bookstore owner Kathleen Kelly (Meg Ryan) regularly interacts over the Internet with superstore head Joe Fox (Tom Hanks). The anonymity of Internet interactions disguises their identities. Kathleen eventually meets Joe Fox, but still does not know that he is the same person she interacts with over the Internet. Joe Fox also does not know that Kathleen is his Internet partner. This is a charming, warm remake of *The Shop Around the Corner* (1940).

Scenes

There are two scenes that offer strong contrasts in social interaction. The first scenes show Internet interaction. The second shows face-to-face interaction. Try to predict their face-to-face interaction before watching the second scene.

1.   Start: 0:04:34 — Stop: 0:09:43 — 5 minutes

These scenes start as Frank (Greg Kinnear) leaves for work. Kathleen comes out of the bathroom and logs on to America Online. They end as Joe Fox enters a shrouded building—the site of his new superstore.

2.   Start: 0:33:35 — Stop: 0:39:23 — 6 minutes

These scenes start with Frank's voiceover saying, "A nut. She called me a nut?" Frank and Kathleen are walking in the evening to the party. The scenes end as the two couples separate and Joe says, "Hey hon', have you ever had a caviar garnish?"

What to Watch for and Ask Yourself

- What effects does anonymity have on their Internet interactions?
- Do you expect their face-to-face interaction to differ in quality? Why?
- Do anonymous Internet interactions have the same effects in organizations?

Concepts or Examples

☐ Email interaction   ☐ Anonymity

☐ Internet interaction   ☐ Face-to-face interaction

☐ Nonverbal communication

Analysis

_____

_____

_____

_____

_____

Personal Reactions

_____

_____

_____

_____

_____

References

Cairncross, F. 1998. *The Death of Distance*. Boston: Harvard Business School Press.

Gross, N. and O. Port. 1998. The Next WAVE. *Business Week* (August 31): 80: 82–83.

Quain, J. R. 1998. How to Shop for a Palmtop. *Fast Company* (September): 196–203.

CHAPTER 5

International Context

The global environment of organizations demands that modern managers have an international focus. Now, the world is their environment and will become increasingly so in the future. For some organizations, thinking internationally means finding new markets outside the home country; for others, becoming a multinational organization operating in many countries; and for others becoming a transnational organization whose decisions are not limited by country boundaries. Modern managers must think of the entire planet as a source of labor and materials, places of production, and markets (Johnston 1991; Kirkland 1988).

Regional trade agreements are opening vast new markets, possibly increasing the competition faced by a firm (Aho and Ostry 1990; Ostry 1990). The North American Free Trade Agreement (NAFTA) of 1994 opened the borders of Mexico, Canada, and the United States to easy movement of goods, capital, and services (Davis and Calmes 1993). Europe took similar steps to encourage freer trade among its countries. The movement of eleven European countries to a single currency, the Euro (€), should enhance freer trade among its users (Fox 1998).

The movie scenes described in this chapter will help introduce you to the global environment of organizations. The selected scenes come from the following films:

- French Kiss
- Tampopo (Dandelion)
- Mississippi Masala
- Ciao, Professore!

French Kiss shows a stereotypical view of the French. *Tampopo (Dandelion)*, a Japanese film, has a satirical view of Japanese eating styles, conformity, and deviant behavior. *Mississippi Masala* offers a view of East Indian culture. *Ciao, Professore!*, an Italian film, offers some observations on Italian culture.

French Kiss

Color, 1995
Running Time: 1 hour, 51 minutes
Rating: PG-13
Distributor: *PolyGram Filmed Entertainment*

Jilted Kate (Meg Ryan) goes to Paris to pursue her fiancée. Although frightened of flying, Kate gets the support of Luc (Kevin Kline), a French thief. Kate's stereotype of French men rules her behavior, but she and Luc eventually develop a close relationship. This is a light, charming film with many wonderful scenes of France.

Scenes (Start: 0:35:59 — Stop: 0:39:29 — 3 minutes)

These scenes start as Kate and Luc leave a hotel in a hurry. Luc says, "All right. All right. You wait here. I'll go get my car." They end after Luc drives the car over the curb and stops. Kate says, "I didn't beg." Luc responds, "No, but you fainted." Then he gets out and flips off the two pedestrians.

What to Watch for and Ask Yourself

- Which parts of this sequence give you the most contrast with your home culture?
- Do you feel there is accurate portrayal of at least some Frenchmen's behavior? Why or why not?
- Are there any implications of these scenes for a foreigner entering a new culture?

Concepts or Examples

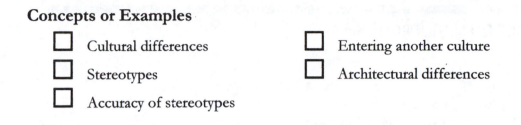

☐ Cultural differences   ☐ Entering another culture

☐ Stereotypes   ☐ Architectural differences

☐ Accuracy of stereotypes

Analysis

_____

_____

_____

_____

_____

Personal Reactions

_____

_____

_____

_____

_____

Tampopo (Dandelion)

Color, 1986
Japanese with English subtitles
Running Time: 1 hour, 54 minutes
Rating: No rating
Distributor: *Republic Pictures Home Video*

A satire that offers an irreverent look at several aspects of Japanese society, especially the role of food and various eating habits. Truck driver Goro (Tsutomu Yamazaki) tries to help Tampopo (Nobuko Miyamoto) develop a successful noodle shop. This film was popular among the Japanese, suggesting it showed the reality of their society from a fresh viewpoint.

Scenes (Start: 0:22:44 — Stop: 0:30:34 — 8 minutes)

This sequence starts as Tampopo cools down after jogging while Goro sits on his bicycle blowing a whistle. The subtitle reads, "Why am I doing this?" Several businessmen come down the stairs and go to a restaurant. The sequence ends as the camera pans away from the young women eating noodles with great zest and noise.

What to Watch for and Ask Yourself

- Which aspects of Japanese culture did you immediately notice while viewing this sequence?
- What was your reaction to the behavior of the businessmen in the restaurant?
- How do you believe you would feel if you were in a restaurant in Japan and observed these people eating noodles?

Concepts or Examples

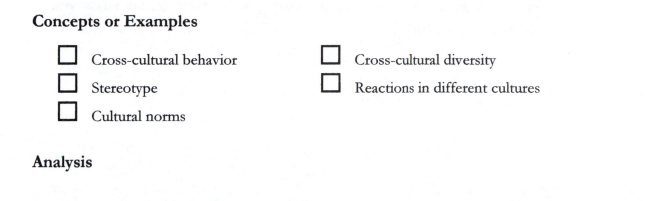

☐ Cross-cultural behavior   ☐ Cross-cultural diversity

☐ Stereotype   ☐ Reactions in different cultures

☐ Cultural norms

Analysis

_____

_____

_____

_____

_____

_____

Personal Reactions

_____

_____

_____

_____

_____

_____

Mississippi Masala

Color, 1992
Running Time: 1 hour, 58 minutes
Rating: R
Distributor: *Columbia TriStar Home Video*

A warm, engaging story about interracial romance between an African-American man and an East Indian woman. The film traces the effects on Indian families after their ouster from Idi Amin's Uganda and their move to Greenwood, Mississippi. Several scenes offer stunning glimpses of Indian culture.

Scene (Start: 0:29:03 — Stop: 0:31:46 — 3 minutes)

The scene starts with the shot of a lighted motel sign that reads, "Hotel Monte Cristo." Some letters are not lit. They end as Mina (Sarita Choudhury) and Harry Patel (Ashok Lath) leave the wedding reception. The movie cuts to the motel reception desk.

What to Watch for and Ask Yourself

- Which aspects of East Indian culture captured your attention while viewing the scene?
- Did the scene show any values that are important in Indian culture?
- Do you now feel that you understand some limited aspects of East Indian culture?

Concepts or Examples

☐ Cross-cultural experience

☐ Physical characteristics of culture

☐ Cultural values

☐ Stereotypes

☐ Understanding other cultures

☐ Cross-cultural diversity

Analysis

_____

_____

_____

_____

_____

Personal Reactions

_____

_____

_____

_____

_____

Ciao, Professore!

Color, 1992
Italian with English subtitles.
Running Time: 1 hour, 31 minutes
Rating: R
Distributor: *Miramax Home Entertainment*

Lina Wertmuller's charming film shows the relationships that develop between a school teacher and his elementary school students. An administrative error mistakenly transfers Marco Tulio Sperelli (Paolo Villagio) to a run-down school in Southern Italy. Set in a small town near Naples, he tries to change the lives of his students and undergoes change himself.

Scenes (Start: 0:05:09 — Stop: 0:15:46 — 11 minutes)

These scenes begin the film. They start with a shot of a ship in a bay and Sperelli driving along the bay while listening to Louis Armstrong. The sequence ends after Sperelli finishes talking to the janitor and he leaves the school. The movie cuts to him walking toward a cafe.

What to Watch for and Ask Yourself

- What aspects of Italian culture appear in these scenes?
- Is Italian culture the same throughout the country?
- Using the experience of these scenes, would you like to visit Italy?

Concepts or Examples

☐ Culture

☐ Physical characteristics of culture

☐ Foreign language

☐ Stories and parables

☐ Cultural differences

☐ Cultural values

Analysis

_____

_____

_____

_____

_____

Personal Reactions

_____

_____

_____

_____

_____

References

Aho, C. M., and S. Ostry. 1990. Regional Trading Blocs: Pragmatic or Problematic Policy? In *The Global Economy: America's Role in the Decade Ahead,* ed. W. E. Brock and R. D. Hormats. New York: W. W. Norton, 147–173.

Davis, B., and J. Calmes. 1993. The House Passes Nafta—Trade Win: House Approves Nafta, Providing President With Crucial Victory. *Wall Street Journal* (November18): A1.

Fox, J. 1998. Europe Is Heading for a Wild Ride. *Fortune* (August 17): 145–146, 148–149.

Johnston, W. B. 1991. Global Workforce 2000: The New Labor Market. *Harvard Business Review* 69: 115–129.

Kirkland, Jr., R. I. 1988. Entering a New Age of Boundless Competition. *Fortune* (14 March): 40–48.

Ostry, S. 1990. Governments and Corporations in a Shrinking World: Trade and Innovation Policies in the United States, Europe, and Japan. *Columbia Journal of World Business* 25: 10–16.

Ethics and Social Responsibility

Ethical behavior is behavior viewed as right and honorable. Unethical behavior is viewed as wrong and reprehensible. These straightforward definitions raise tough questions for managers and their organizations. First, what standards should they use to judge behavior as ethical or unethical? Second, how should the adjectives used to distinguish ethical from unethical behavior be defined? *Right* and *wrong* have different meanings to different people. Standards of ethical behavior also vary from one country to another (Brandt 1959; Buchholz 1989, Ch. 1).

Social responsibility of organizations emphasizes the effects of management decisions on the organization's external environment. It asks managers to consider the social and environmental effects of decisions, not only the economic effects (Wood 1991).

Questions of ethics and social responsibility abound in organizations and affect management decisions. Is it ethical for an organization to withhold product safety information? Is it ethical for a person to use knowledge about human perception to affect the perception of an organization's customers or employees? Is it ethical for an organization to refuse to continuously improve the quality of its products or services when customers do not demand it? Those are only three ethical questions from an almost endless list that managers face.

The following films show ethics and behavior in organizations:

- Grumpier Old Men
- The Godfather
- Other People's Money
- Scent of a Woman

The lighter side of an ethical dilemma appears in *Grumpier Old Men*. *The Godfather* offers dramatic—and violent—observations on ethical dilemmas. *Other People's Money* has a scene in which two people persuade shareholders to accept their proposals—an example of ethics in the context of persuasive communication. The scenes from *Scent of a Women* are outstanding demonstrations of the meaning of ethical behavior.

Grumpier Old Men

Color, 1995
Running Time: 1 hour, 41 minutes
Rating: PG-13
Distributor: *Warner Home Video*

This is the sequel to *Grumpy Old Men,* featuring the same two grumps: Max Goldman (Walter Matthau) and John Gustafson (Jack Lemmon). It is a light-hearted comedy showing the lifelong relationship two next-door neighbors. They constantly argue and insult each other but are actually good friends, especially when fishing. Their lifelong goal has been to catch the biggest catfish in the lake, "Catfish Hunter."

Scenes (Start: 1:27:05 — Stop: 1:33:42 — 7 minutes)

These scenes start as Max and John walk to their car and prepare to drive to the church for Max's wedding. They end as Max realizes he and John are late for his wedding, race the boat to shore, and drive to the church. Max sings a verse from "Get Me to the Church on Time."

What to Watch for and Ask Yourself

- Do Max and John face a moral dilemma? How many?
- What ethical guidelines do they use to decide a course of action?
- Do they behave ethically or unethically?

Concepts or Examples

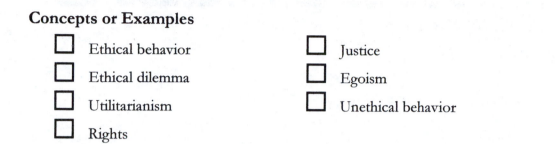

☐ Ethical behavior

☐ Ethical dilemma

☐ Utilitarianism

☐ Rights

☐ Justice

☐ Egoism

☐ Unethical behavior

Analysis

_____

_____

_____

_____

_____

Personal Reactions

_____

_____

_____

_____

_____

The Godfather (I)

Color, 1972
Running Time: 2 hour, 51 minutes
Rating: R
Distributor: *Paramount Pictures Corp.*

This is a powerful look at a Mafia family led by Don Corleone (Marlon Brando) based on the novel by Mario Puzo. This intense film roams through the personal lives of its characters and shows the fiercely violent side of organized crime. An irresistible work, *The Godfather* is filled with memorable scenes and memorable performances. Other scenes from this film are discussed on pages 168 and 184.

Scenes (Tape 2. Start: 0:40:24 — Stop: 0:45:25 — 5 minutes)

This sequence, which follows the scenes of Don Corleone's funeral, starts inside a church with the sound of a baby crying and organ music playing. It ends after the priest says to Michael Corleone (Al Pacino), the son of the Don, "Michael Brizzi. Go in peace and may the lord be with you. Amen." The movie cuts to outside the church with church bells ringing. The baby in this baptismal scene is director Francis Ford Coppola's infant daughter.

What to Watch for and Ask Yourself

- What ethical dilemmas does Michael face in these scenes?
- How does he manage his way through them?
- Are such dilemmas a believable part of modern life? Try to recall some examples from your experience.

Concepts or Examples

☐ Ethical behavior

☐ Unethical behavior

☐ Legal behavior

☐ Ethical dilemmas

☐ Illegal dilemmas

Analysis

_____

_____

_____

_____

_____

Personal Reactions

_____

_____

_____

_____

_____

Other People's Money

Color, 1991
Running Time: 1 hour, 51 minutes
Rating: R
Distributor: *Warner Home Video*

Lawrence Garfield (Danny DeVito) is a strong-willed Wall Street investment banker with a reputation for buying and liquidating companies. He sets out to acquire New England Wire & Cable Company. The 86-year-old company in a small Rhode Island town is the main source of employment for the townspeople. Although other divisions of the company are profitable, the wire and cable division is losing money. Chairman of the Board Andrew Jorgenson (Gregory Peck) has deep personal ties to the company his father founded. He also has a deep commitment to his employees and tries to fight Garfield's takeover effort.

Scenes (Start: 1:17:28 — Stop: 1:34:46 — 17 minutes)

This sequence begins with the wide shot of the plant and Garfield arriving in his limousine for the shareholders' meeting. It ends after Garfield stares forlornly at Kate Sullivan (Penelope Ann Miller) as she walks away and his limousine leaves the plant. The film cuts to a night shot of Manhattan.

These scenes are at the end of the film, after Garfield has had an extended personal and legal fight with Kate Sullivan, the daughter of Jorgenson's wife. He also has fallen in love with her and has asked her to marry him. She has not responded to his advances.

Garfield had presented his financial analysis to Jorgenson earlier in the film, trying to persuade him to sell the company. His analysis showed:

Salvage value of plant and equipment	$30 million
Land value	$10 million
Value of other divisions	$60 million
Working capital	$25 million
Total	**$125 million**

Garfield offered a conservative estimate of the sale value as $100 million.

What to Watch for and Ask Yourself

- Which ethical theory dominates Jorgenson's arguments?
- Which ethical theory dominates Garfield's arguments?
- Do the stockholders make an ethical or unethical decision? Why or why not?

Concepts or Examples

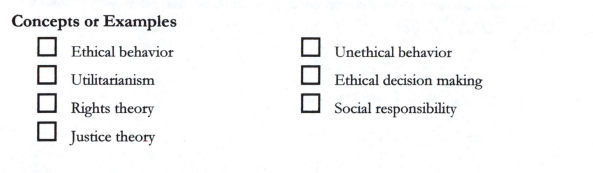

☐ Ethical behavior   ☐ Unethical behavior

☐ Utilitarianism   ☐ Ethical decision making

☐ Rights theory   ☐ Social responsibility

☐ Justice theory

Analysis

_____

_____

_____

_____

_____

Personal Reactions

_____

_____

_____

_____

_____

Scent of a Woman

Color, 1992
Running Time: 2 hour, 37 minutes
Rating: R
Distributor: *MCA Universal Home Video*

Young Charlie Simms (Chris O'Donnell) tries to earn extra money over a week-end by working as a guide and caretaker for the ill-tempered, retired, and blind Lieutenant Colonel Frank Slade (Al Pacino). Charlie is quiet, reserved, and has had little experience with the opposite sex while attending an exclusive preparatory school on a scholarship. His wild weekend with the Colonel bonds them forever.

Charlie and another student, George Willis, Jr. (Philip S. Hoffman), had seen three students vandalize the headmaster's new Jaguar. Under repeated questioning by the headmaster, neither Charlie nor George identified the students. The headmaster pressures Charlie by noting that his career depends on the headmaster's support for him to go to Harvard University. George's father (Baxter Harris), a big donor, pressures George to identify the students so George will suffer no negative effects.

Scenes (Start: 2:09:20 — Stop: 2:29:06 — 20 minutes)

The sequence starts with Charlie Simms saying good-bye to the Colonel in the limousine. It ends after Charlie and the Colonel leave the chapel surrounded by cheering students. These scenes are the joint faculty-student hearing called by Mr. Trask (James Rebhorn), the headmaster, to settle the matter and decide the fate of Charlie and George.

What to Watch for and Ask Yourself

- Does George Willis, Jr. behave ethically or unethically?
- Does Charlie Simms behave ethically or unethically?
- Do the others in these scenes behave ethically or unethically?

Concepts or Examples

☐ Ethical behavior   ☐ Rights

☐ Unethical behavior   ☐ Justice

☐ Utilitarianism   ☐ Role of integrity in leadership

Analysis

_____

_____

_____

_____

_____

_____

Personal Reactions

_____

_____

_____

_____

_____

References

Brandt, R. B. 1959. *Ethical Theory: The Problems of Normative and Critical Ethics.* Englewood Cliffs, NJ: Prentice Hall.

Buchholz, R. A. 1989. *Fundamental Concepts and Problems in Business Ethics.* Englewood Cliffs, NJ: Prentice Hall.

Wood, D. J. 1991. Corporate Social Performance Revisited. *Academy of Management Review* 16: 691–718.

Problem Solving

Problems occur in organizations when actual situations do not match a desired state (Lyles and Mitroff 1980; Pounds 1969). Examples of common organizational problems include over and understaffing, dealing with inventory shortages, and resolving customer complaints. Managers can also frame problems as opportunities. A series of customer complaints that focus on common issues can present managers with an opportunity to improve processes.

Problem-solving processes in organizations focus on finding the root causes of the problem. Along with decision-making processes, they are a complex collection of processes used by both managers and nonmanagers. Problem solving identifies a problem and searches for root causes. The process creates options or alternatives that enter a decision-making process. Managers use the latter process to choose among the options.

Several films offer effective scenes showing problem solving. This chapter discusses problem-solving scenes from the following films:

- Apollo 13
- The Rock
- James and the Giant Peach
- Papillon

Apollo 13 focuses on problem solving— the problem of the safe return of the astronauts in their damaged space capsule. *The Rock* has a powerful scene of problem solving involving a lethal gas. *James and the Giant Peach* has a beautifully animated sequence that shows some complex aspects of problem solving and its links to decision making. The closing scenes of *Papillon* dramatically show how Papillon solved his problem—escaping Devil's Island.

Apollo 13 (I)

Color, 1995
Distributor: 2 hours, 20 minutes
Rating: PG
Distributor: *MCA Universal Home Video*

This film dramatically portrays the Apollo 13 mission to the moon that almost had an in-space disaster. Innovative problem solving and decision making amid massive ambiguity saved the crew. The film is filled with examples of both problem solving and decision making. Almost any set of scenes dramatically makes the point. Another scene from *Apollo 13* is discussed on page 82.

Scenes

There are two scenes at different points in the film. The first shows the engineers working on the problem. The second shows the astronauts working on the problem.

1. Start: 1:20:57 — Stop: 1:22:02 — 1 minute

The scene starts with a wide shot of the Earth–Moon Transit control board in Mission Control. Three men enter and go to flight director Gene Kranz (Ed Harris). One says, "Gene, we have a situation brewing with the carbon dioxide." It ends after the engineers start organizing the material. The movie cuts to a television set showing old tape of the astronauts.

2. Start: 1:29:04 — Stop: 1:33:56 — 5 minutes

The second scene starts with the engineer carrying the filter down the hall to mission control. It ends after a controller says, "That is good to hear Aquarius. And you Sir are a steely-eyed missile man." The movie cuts to an astronaut in a simulator.

What to Watch for and Ask Yourself

- What is the problem in these scenes?
- What are the engineers' options for solving the problem?
- Are the astronauts doing problem solving or decision making?

Concepts or Examples

☐ Problem solving   ☐ Options

☐ Problem identification   ☐ Decision making

☐ Root causes

Analysis

_____

_____

_____

_____

_____

_____

Personal Reactions

_____

_____

_____

_____

_____

The Rock

Color, 1996
Running Time: 2 hours, 16 minutes
Rating: R
Distributor: *Hollywood Pictures Home Video*

A disgruntled Marine general (Ed Harris) takes over Alcatraz and threatens to fire rockets with a deadly gas into San Francisco. A previously imprisoned British agent (Sean Connery), the only person to escape from Alcatraz, teams with FBI biochemist Stanley Goodspeed (Nicolas Cage) to lead a team into the prison. Almost continuous action heightens the suspense as the film takes many twists and turns to its conclusion.

Scene (Start: 0:16:25 — Stop: 0:21:17 — 5 minutes)

This scene begins with an aerial shot of the FBI Laboratory, Washington, DC. It ends after Goodspeed tells his girlfriend about his day. She goes on to tell him she is pregnant. The scene has R-rated language.

What to Watch for and Ask Yourself

- Do these scenes show decision making or problem solving?
- Does Goodspeed have many solutions to the problem or only a few?
- Did Goodspeed's biochemistry knowledge help him choose the right solution?

Concepts or Examples

☐ Decision making   ☐ Solution generation

☐ Problem solving   ☐ Solution choice

☐ Problem analysis   ☐ Expert knowledge

Analysis

_____

_____

_____

_____

_____

_____

Personal Reactions

_____

_____

_____

_____

_____

_____

James and the Giant Peach (II)

Color, 1996
Running Time: 1 hour, 19 minutes
Rating: G
Distributor: *Walt Disney Home Video*

This enchanting adaptation of Roald Dahl's novel is described in more detail in another scene discussion on page 16.

Scenes (Start: 0:33:34 — Stop: 0:42:52 — 9 minutes)

This sequence starts after the peach lands in the ocean. It begins with a dark screen and a dark inside shot. You hear, "Ow. Somebody pinched me." Centipede says, "Sorry, I thought you were the spider." It ends after Centipede says, "New York, here we come." The peach rises out of the ocean.

What to Watch for and Ask Yourself

- What is the problem or problems facing this group?
- What alternatives are available to them to solve the problem?
- Does their diversity help or hinder their problem solving?

Concepts or Examples

☐ Problem solving

☐ Innovation

☐ Diversity and group performance

☐ Problem-solving group

Analysis

_____

_____

_____

_____

_____

_____

Personal Reactions

_____

_____

_____

_____

_____

Papillon

Color, 1973
Running Time: 2 hours, 30 minutes
Rating: PG
Distributor: *Warner Home Video*

This is Dalton Trumbo and Lorenzo Semple Jr.'s fine adaptation of the auto-biographical account of Henri Charriere's repeated efforts to escape from the French prison colony on Devil's Island in the 1930s. Charriere, known as Papillon ("the butterfly"), focused all his efforts on leaving the island, something no prisoner had ever done.

Scenes (Start: 2:17:02 — Stop: 2:28:28 — 11 minutes)

Papillon (Steve McQueen) has finished his prison sentence and is living on the island. He met former prisoner Luis Dega (Dustin Hoffman) before these scenes start.

The scenes start with the shot of the surf breaking against the base of a cliff. The camera pans to Papillon holding a coconut and looking at the water. The scenes end after he floats away from the island and you hear the voice-over, "Papillon made it to freedom. And for the remaining years of his life he lived a free man." Movie cuts to scene of abandoned prison building.

What to Watch for and Ask Yourself

- What is the problem facing Papillon?
- What alternatives are available to him to solve the problem?
- Which decision model or models best describe Papillon's decision process?

Concepts or Examples

☐ Problem solving ☐ Rational model

☐ Decision making ☐ Garbage can model

☐ Decision alternatives ☐ Bounded rationality model

☐ Decision-making process

Analysis

_____

_____

_____

_____

_____

Personal Reactions

_____

_____

_____

_____

_____

References

Lyles, M. A., and I. I. Mitroff. 1980. Organizational Problem Formulation: An Empirical Study. *Administrative Science Quarterly* 25: 102–119.

Pounds, W. E. The Process of Problem Finding. 1969. *Industrial Management Review* 11: 1–19.

CHAPTER 9

Decision Making

The **decision-making process** has three steps: defining a decision problem; creating alternative courses of action; and choosing among them using specified or unspecified criteria. The criteria for choosing among alternatives can include the cost, profit, danger, or pleasure of each alternative. Although decision making focuses on choice, it also intends to reach a goal (Wilson and Alexis 1962).

Decision making fits within the larger context of problem-solving activities in organizations. Individuals in organizations, especially managers, face problems, opportunities, and events requiring action. Problem solving identifies the problem, tries to find root causes, and creates the options that become the input to a decision-making process. Decision making is the part of the problem-solving process that chooses a course of action (Huber 1980).

Although decision making is a basic management function, nonmanagers also make decisions (Barnard 1938). The term *decision maker* refers to a person at any level in an organization who picks a course of action when faced with a decision situation.

Four films discussed in this chapter offer effective scenes that show different aspects of decision making:

- Apollo 13
- Butch Cassidy and the Sundance Kid
- My Best Friend's Wedding
- Network

Apollo 13 has some superb scenes that show decision making. *Butch Cassidy and the Sundance Kid* shows a major decision being made about whether to fight the posse or jump off a cliff into a river. *My Best Friend's Wedding* shows the stress of the decision-making process. A closing scene from *Network* shows group decision making in action with unexpected results.

Apollo 13 (II)

Color, 1995
Running Time: 2 hours, 20 minutes
Rating: PG
Distributor: *MCA Universal Home Video*

This film recreates the heroic effort of astronaut Jim Lovell, his crew, NASA, and Mission Control to return their damaged Apollo spacecraft back to Earth. Examples of both problem solving and decision making take place in almost every scene. See page 72 for more information about this film and an additional scene discussion.

Scene (Start: 1:16:04 — Stop: 1:18:04 — 2 minutes)

This scene starts as Flight Director Gene Kranz (Ed Harris) reaches for chalk and writes on the board. He says, "So you are telling me you can only give our guys forty-five hours." It ends as he leaves the room saying, "Failure is not an option."

What to Watch for and Ask Yourself

- Does this scene show problem solving or decision making?
- Where is the separation between the two?
- Are these largely individual or group decision processes?

Concepts or Examples

☐ Problem solving

☐ Decision making

☐ Decision-making models

☐ Individual decision making

☐ Group decision making

Analysis

_____

_____

_____

_____

_____

_____

Personal Reactions

_____

_____

_____

_____

_____

Butch Cassidy and the Sundance Kid (I)

Color, 1969
Running Time: 1 hour, 12 minutes
Rating: PG
Distributor: *Fox Video*

This seriocomic Western takes liberties with the lives of two real-life train robbers in the 1890s. It has many memorable scenes, including a bicycle riding scene that showcases Burt Bacharach's Oscar-winning song, "Raindrops Keep Fallin' On My Head." Much happens along the way as the posse chases the pair, who eventually fight a large group of Bolivian police. Other scenes from this film are discussed on pages 112 and 244.

Scenes (Start: 0:53:02 — Stop: 1:02:56 — 10 minutes)

These scenes start with Butch Cassidy (Paul Newman) and Sundance (Robert Redford) riding on the same horse to escape a posse in hot pursuit. The movie cuts to Butch falling into some water to cool off. He says, "Ah, you're wasting your time. "They can't track us over rock." Sundance replies, "Tell them that." They end as the two of them float down the river in the distance. The movie cuts to a shot of Etta Place (Katherine Ross) sitting on a porch. Butch and Sundance approach the house.

What to Watch for and Ask Yourself

- Which model of decision making do Butch and Sundance appear to follow?
- What alternatives do they assess in reaching a decision?
- Was their decision the right one under these circumstances?

Concepts or Examples

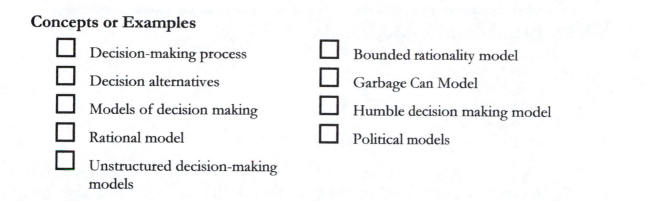

☐ Decision-making process

☐ Decision alternatives

☐ Models of decision making

☐ Rational model

☐ Unstructured decision-making models

☐ Bounded rationality model

☐ Garbage Can Model

☐ Humble decision making model

☐ Political models

Analysis

_____

_____

_____

_____

_____

_____

Personal Reactions

_____

_____

_____

_____

_____

My Best Friend's Wedding (II)

Color, 1997
Running Time: 1 hour, 45 minutes
Rating: PG-13
Distributor: *Columbia TriStar Home Video*

This modern comedy of errors was a box office hit. It comes to a climax when true love wins out in the end. For another scene and a description of this film, see page 36.

Scene (Start: 1:06:52 — Stop: 1:11:22 — 4 minutes)

This scene starts with Julianne (Julia Roberts) walking down a hall toward a conference room. They follow the barge on the Chicago River scene. She asks Walter Wallace (Philip Bosco) if she can use his office telephone. It ends with Wallace saying goodbye to his secretary and walks toward Julianne waiting at the elevators. The film cuts to Michael and Julianne trying to insert keys into the front door of the Wallace building.

Alternate stopping points:

1. 1:12:22. Julianne is starring into the lobby of the Wallace building.
2. 1:18:05. Close-up shot of Michael saying, "I am crazy ... to fall for someone I hardly knew.

What to Watch for and Ask Yourself

- What decision alternatives did Julianne have?
- What were her decision criteria?
- What effects do you predict from her decision?

Concepts or Examples

☐ Decision-making process   ☐ Decision criteria

☐ Decisions and stress   ☐ Effects of the decision

☐ Decision alternatives

Analysis

_____

_____

_____

_____

_____

Personal Reactions

_____

_____

_____

_____

_____

Network (I)

Color, 1976
Running Time: 1 hour, 56 minutes
Rating: R
Distributor: *MGM/UA Home Video*

Union Broadcasting Systems (UBS) fires news anchor Howard Beale (Peter Finch) because of poor ratings. Max Schumacher (William Holden), the news division head, tries to soften the blow on Beale. Beale's on-air behavior then becomes increasingly bizarre after he promises to kill himself on live television—a promise that eventually makes his show a winner. Over the course of two weeks, its ratings skyrocket, something UBS management values over human life. The celebrated screenwriter Paddy Chayefsky wrote this scathing satire of the television industry. Another scene is discussed on page 276.

Scene (Start: 1:48:53 — Stop: 1:53:36 — 5 minutes)

The scene begins with the network executives coming into Frank Hackett's office. Hackett (Robert Duvall) sits at his desk. The scene ends after Diana Christensen (Faye Dunaway) says, "I don't see we have any option, Frank. Let's kill the son of a bitch." The film intercuts several shots of the audience going into the studio

What to Watch for and Ask Yourself

- What decision alternatives do these network executives have?
- Which decision model guided them to a final decision?
- Was their decision ethical, unethical, legal, or illegal?

Concepts or Examples

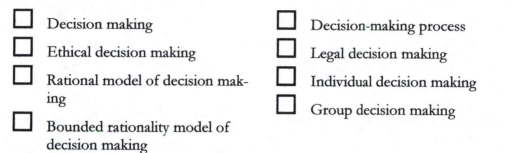

☐ Decision making

☐ Ethical decision making

☐ Rational model of decision making

☐ Bounded rationality model of decision making

☐ Decision-making process

☐ Legal decision making

☐ Individual decision making

☐ Group decision making

Analysis

_____

_____

_____

_____

_____

_____

Personal Reactions

_____

_____

_____

_____

_____

_____

References

Barnard, C. I. 1938. *The Functions of the Executive*. Cambridge, MA: Harvard University Press.

Huber, G. P. 1980. *Managerial Decision Making*. Glenview, IL: Scott, Foresman and Company.

Wilson, C. Z., and M. Alexis. 1962. Basic Frameworks for Decisions. *Academy of Management Journal* 5: 150–164.

Organizing: Existing and Evolving Organizational Forms

Organizational design refers to the way managers structure their organization to reach the organization's goals. The allocation of duties, tasks, and responsibilities between departments and individuals is an element of organizational design. Reporting relationships and the number of levels in the organization's hierarchy are other structural elements (Banner and Gagne 1995; Butler 1991; Davis and Weckler 1996; Flamholtz and Randle 1998; Nadler and Tushman 1997).

Organizational charts show the formal design of an organization. They show the configuration of the organization as it is or as managers would like it to be. Such charts typically use boxes to show positions in the organization and lines connecting the boxes to show reporting relationships (White 1963).

An organization's design has two goals. It must get information to the right places for effective decision making, and it must help coordinate the interdependent parts of the organization. When the organization's design is not right for what it is doing, managers may not get the information they need to predict problems and make effective decisions (Duncan 1979). They also may not react quickly enough to problems because the existing organizational design blocks needed information. Conflict levels in the organization could be excessively high, implying misalignments in the organization's design.

This chapter discusses scenes from the following films:

- The River Wild
- The Hudsucker Proxy
- The Hunt for Red October
- The Dirty Dozen

Whitewater river rafting scenes from *The River Wild* are excellent visual metaphors of a turbulent external environment. *The Hudsucker Proxy* shows a functional organizational design in action. *The Hunt for Red October* shows different functional areas of a submarine working to reach its mission. *The Dirty Dozen* effectively depicts strategy formation and a resulting organizational design.

The River Wild

Color, 1994
Running Time: 1 hour, 52 minutes
Rating: PG-13
Distributor: *MCA Universal Home Video*

Two crooks, psychopath Wade (Kevin Bacon) and his partner Terry (John C. Riley), start down the river in a rubber raft. A chance meeting with Gail (Meryl Streep) and her family changes the family's vacation dramatically. Wade has a gun but quickly learns that he and Terry must depend on Gail, an experienced river guide, to safely traverse the rapids. The most challenging stretch of rapids is "the Gauntlet," the convergence of three rivers and a drop of 295 feet in one and a half miles.

Scenes (Start: 1:38:28 — Stop: 1:45:15 — 7 minutes)

This sequence starts as the raft enters the Gauntlet. Gail says, "The vacation is over." It ends after they pass through the last rapids and shout, "We made it."

What to Watch for and Ask Yourself

- What type of environment do the four people in the raft face?
- Did their environment change as they went through the Gauntlet?
- If so, did they change their organizational design?

Concepts or Examples

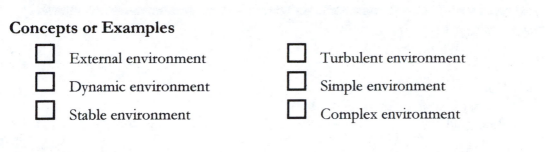

☐ External environment ☐ Turbulent environment

☐ Dynamic environment ☐ Simple environment

☐ Stable environment ☐ Complex environment

Analysis

_____

_____

_____

_____

_____

_____

Personal Reactions

_____

_____

_____

_____

_____

The Hudsucker Proxy (I)

Color, 1994
Rating: 1 hour, 51 minutes
Rating: PG
Distributor: *Warner Home Video*

Norville Barnes (Tim Robbins), a graduate of the Muncie College of Business Administration, quickly moves from mailroom clerk to President of Hudsucker Industries. The board of directors appoints him in the hope that his incompetence will drive down the stock price so they can buy a controlling interest. Norville has his own idea for a product, a simple plastic hoop. After a slow start in sales, the hula-hoop becomes a success, drives the stock price up, and causes the board great distress. Sidney J. Mossberger (Paul Newman) aspires to the presidency and sabotages Norville by presenting him as insane. The film takes a delightful twist at the end when Norville inherits the late Waring Hudsucker's fortune, regains the presidency, and presents the board with a new product idea—the Frisbee.

Another scene from this film is discussed on page 194.

Scenes (Start: 1:03:17 — Stop: 1:08:03 — 5 minutes)

These scenes begin with the shot of the board meeting session sign on a door. It ends after the hula-hoop sign appears in a toy store window, and the storeowner steps outside.

What to Watch for and Ask Yourself

- Which types of organizational design does this scene show?
- Which characteristics of organizational design are shown in the scene?
- Does the scene show any behavioral demands of organizational design? What are they?

Concepts or Examples

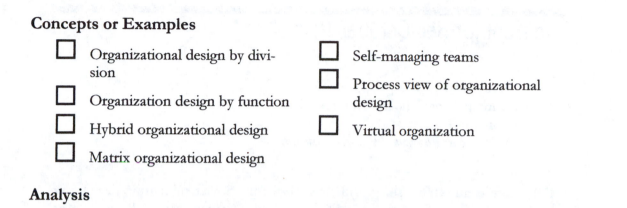

☐ Organizational design by division

☐ Organization design by function

☐ Hybrid organizational design

☐ Matrix organizational design

☐ Self-managing teams

☐ Process view of organizational design

☐ Virtual organization

Analysis

_____

_____

_____

_____

_____

Personal Reactions

_____

_____

_____

_____

_____

The Hunt for Red October (I)

Color, 1990
Running Time: 2 hours, 15 minutes
Rating: PG
Distributor: *Paramount Pictures Corporation*

This film is an intense story of the search for the Soviet submarine *Red October*. Contradictory information says its commander Captain Marko Ramius (Sean Connery) is either defecting to the United States or has gone berserk and will unleash nuclear missiles on the U.S. The Soviets want the U.S. to find the *Red October* and destroy it. Intelligence agent Jack Ryan (Alec Baldwin) believes Ramius wants to defect and does not want him killed. Another discussion of this film can be found on page 188.

Scenes Start: 1:29:03 — Stop: 1:38:57 — 10 minutes)

These scenes start with the Russian Ambassador (Joss Ackland) saying to the President's National Security Adviser (Richard Jordan), "I have to talk to the President." They follow the scenes of CIA Analyst Ryan (Alec Baldwin) boarding the submarine *U.S.S. Dallas*. The scenes end after Commander Mancusco (Scott Glen) says, "He wants to go up and take a peek. We'll play along." Both submarines go to the surface. The film cuts to the *Red October* with Captain Ramius (Sean Connery) using the periscope.

What to Watch for and Ask Yourself

- Which forms of organizational design do these scenes show?
- Are the forms clean and pure in practice?
- Did these organizational forms help the two submarines reach their mission?

Concepts or Examples

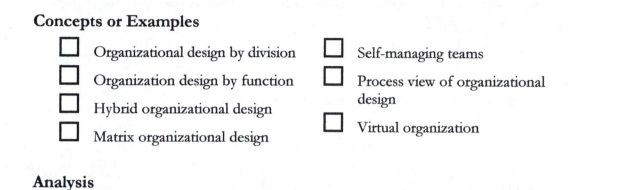

☐ Organizational design by division

☐ Organization design by function

☐ Hybrid organizational design

☐ Matrix organizational design

☐ Self-managing teams

☐ Process view of organizational design

☐ Virtual organization

Analysis

_____

_____

_____

_____

_____

Personal Reactions

_____

_____

_____

_____

_____

The Dirty Dozen (I)

Color, 1967
Running Time: 2 hours, 29 minutes
Rating: NR
Distributor: *MGM/UA Home Video*

Army Major Reisman (Lee Marvin) has the almost impossible task of developing a team of twelve men for action behind the lines against the Germans in World War II. He recruits his men from the murderers, thieves, and rapists in an army prison and makes a deal with them: successfully complete the mission and the Army will commute their sentences. The mission: parachute behind enemy lines at night and blow up a chateau full of German officers before D-Day. Another scene from *The Dirty Dozen* is discussed on page 234.

Scenes

There are two scenes. The first shows Major Reisman (Lee Marvin) going over the mission's plan. The second shows part of the mission underway.

1. Start: 1:41:58 — Stop: 1:44:41 — 3 minutes

The Dirty Dozen has just successfully taken Colonel Breed's (Robert Ryan) headquarters during maneuvers. A sumptuous dinner is their reward. The scene starts with a shot of a barracks and Jimenez (Trini Lopez) banging a spoon on a bottle to get the group's attention. He says, "Hey Major!" It ends after Major Reisman begins another review of the plan and says, "All right, let's take it again from the top without all the ad libs."

2. Start: 2:11:41 — Stop: 2:29:01 — 17 minutes

This sequence starts with Maggott (Telly Savalas) saying with a crazed look on his face, "It's judgment day, you sinners." He has just gleefully killed a German woman. It ends after the operation and a shot of the survivors in their hospital beds.

What to Watch for and Ask Yourself

- Does Major Reisman's strategy lead to a specific organization design? If so, what are its key features?
- What type of environment surrounds The Dirty Dozen while carrying out the strategy?
- Do they adapt their strategic plan while trying to carry it out?

Concepts or Examples

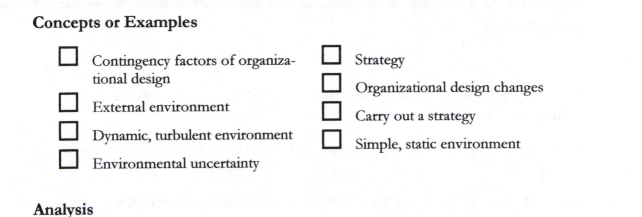

- ☐ Contingency factors of organizational design
- ☐ External environment
- ☐ Dynamic, turbulent environment
- ☐ Environmental uncertainty
- ☐ Strategy
- ☐ Organizational design changes
- ☐ Carry out a strategy
- ☐ Simple, static environment

Analysis

_____

_____

_____

_____

_____

_____

Personal Reactions

_____

_____

_____

_____

_____

References

Banner, D. K., and T. E. Gagne. 1995. *Designing Effective Organizations: Traditional and Transformational Views.* Thousand Oaks, CA: Sage Publications.

Butler, R. J. 1991. *Designing Organizations: A Decision-Making Perspective.* New York: Routledge.

Davis, M. R., and D. A. Weckler. 1996. *A Practical Guide to Organization Design.* Menlo Park, CA: Crisp Publications.

Duncan, R. 1979. What Is the Right Organization Structure? Decision Tree Analysis Provides the answer. *Organizational Dynamics* 7 (Winter): 447–461.

Flamholtz, E. G., and Y. Randle. 1998. *Changing the Game: Organizational Transformations of the First, Second, and Third Kinds.* New York: Oxford University Press.

Nadler, D. A., and M. L. Tushman. 1997. *Competing by Design: The Power of Organizational Architecture.* New York: Oxford University Press.

White, K. K. 1963. *Understanding the Company Organization Chart.* New York: American Management Association.

Human Resource Management:
Job Seeking and Career Management

Human resource management ensures an organization has proper staffing levels to meet the organization's goals (Fisher, Schoenfeldt, and Shaw 1995; Mathis and Jackson 2000). It recruits, selects, socializes, trains, and develops organization members. The human resource management process includes:

1. Human resource planning—assessment of organizational needs, available labor force, and the organization's long-range goals.
2. Recruitment—develop and maintain a pool of job candidates.
3. Selection—choose from the applicant pool to meet organizational needs.
4. Socialization—teach new employees the organization's expectations for behavior and performance. (See also Chapter 20.)
5. Training and development—add to employee skills and prepare employees for future organization jobs.
6. Performance appraisal—assess employee performance against organizational standards.
7. Promotions, transfers, demotions, and separations—managing employee movement within the organization and out of the organization.

This chapter discusses job seeking and career management scenes from the following films:

- Kramer vs. Kramer
- The Freshman
- The Secret of My Success
- The Apartment

Kramer vs. Kramer shows the committed pursuit of a position. *The Freshman* shows a young college student trying to endure a job interview with Marlon Brando's *Godfather* character. *The Secret of My Success* shows contemporary job seeking behavior of a young Kansas college graduate. *The Apartment* has a closing scene depicting the difficulties people can often have in managing their careers.

Kramer vs. Kramer

Color, 1979
Running Time: 1 hour, 45 minutes
Rating: PG
Distributor: *RCA/Columbia Pictures Home Video*

An award winning family drama that shows a father's dilemma after his wife leaves him. Ted Kramer (Dustin Hoffman) must learn to care for his young son while managing the stresses of his job as an advertising executive. His ex-wife Joanna Kramer (Meryl Streep) sues for custody of the son several years after the divorce.

Scenes (Start: 1:01:23 — Stop: 1:07:35 — 6 minutes)

Ted Kramer has just been fired from his job. He desperately needs to find a job before going to court over custody of his son. These scenes start with Kramer playing with his son and Christmas decorations at the kitchen table. The telephone rings and he leaves the table to take the call. They end after he kisses the woman at the Christmas party and says, "Merry Christmas." The film cuts to a guard sitting in a lobby.*

What to Watch for and Ask Yourself

- What is Ted Kramer's job seeking strategy?
- What does he do to impress the manager to hire him?
- What are Kramer's strengths for the position he wants?

---

*Lisa F. Kirby, Coordinator of The Robert O. Anderson School's Placement Office, The University of New Mexico, recommended these scenes. — J.E.C.

Concepts or Examples

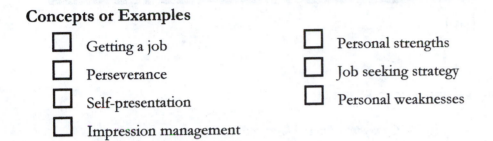

☐ Getting a job   ☐ Personal strengths

☐ Perseverance   ☐ Job seeking strategy

☐ Self-presentation   ☐ Personal weaknesses

☐ Impression management

Analysis

_____

_____

_____

_____

_____

_____

Personal Reactions

_____

_____

_____

_____

_____

The Freshman

Color, 1990
Running Time: 1 hour, 42 minutes
Rating: PG
Distributor: *RCA/Columbia Pictures Home Video*

This charming and satirical film features Matthew Broderick as Clark Kellogg, an aspiring New York University Film student. Shortly after arriving in New York City, Victor Ray (Bruno Kirby) robs him of everything. This encounter leads to Bruno introducing him to his Uncle Carmine (Marlon Brando), an Italian importer-exporter. The resemblance to Marlon Brando's award winning character in *The Godfather* should be apparent.

Scenes (Start: 0:19:40 — Stop: 0:30:04 — 10 minutes)

These scenes show Clark Kellogg interviewing for a job as a runner for Carmine Sabatini. They follow the apartment building roof scene, during which Clark and Victor discussed the theft. Victor suggests he can get Clark a job working for his Uncle. These scenes start with a wide shot of a Manhattan street. Clark Kellogg approaches a restaurant. They end after Carmine leaves the restaurant and the waiter closes the door. The movie cuts to a New York University cinema studies class discussion of *The Godfather*.

What to Watch for and Ask Yourself

- What expectations does Clark Kellogg develop about this job?
- Does he have a realistic impression of what he will do if he accepts the job?
- Does he present himself to Carmine in a positive way?

Concepts or Examples

☐ Job interview ☐ Expectations

☐ Abilities ☐ Self-presentation

☐ Job requirements

Analysis

_____

_____

_____

_____

_____

_____

Personal Reactions

_____

_____

_____

_____

_____

The Secret of My Success (II)

Color, 1987
Running Time: 1 hour, 50 minutes
Rating: PG-13
Distributor: *MCA Home Video*

College graduate Brantley Foster (Michael J. Fox) leaves his Kansas home and goes to New York to look for a job. He is continually frustrated in his quest but lands a mailroom job. An entertaining look at corporate life, this film features power, negotiation, and sexual shenanigans. Another description of this film appears on page 8.

Scenes

Three sets of scenes show job seeking and career management. After viewing set 2, predict whether Brantley's behavior will have positive effects on his career.

1. Start: 0:06:32 — Stop: 0:08:11 — 2 minutes

These scenes start with Brantley Foster looking up at a building saying, "OK New York. If that's the way you want it. OK." They end after Ms. Miller (no name in cast list) says to Brantley, "Can you be a minority woman?" The film cuts to Brantley talking on a public telephone.

2. Start: 1:26:40 — Stop: 1:28:42 — 2 minutes

This set starts with Howard Prescott (Richard Jordan) discussing a report with his staff at his garden party. He says, "Well, I have had a look at the preliminary report. And I am satisfied the proposed cutbacks are our best line of defense." By this time in the film, Brantley also poses as Whitfield, a knowledgeable staff member. The set ends as Vera Prescott smiles (Margaret Whitton). The film cuts to Howard Prescott walking across the lawn, searching for Christy.

3. Start: 1:40:43 — Stop: 1:45:24 — 4 minutes

This set opens with a board and staff meeting discussing the merger proposal from Davenport Industries. Howard Prescott begins the discussions. The set ends after Brantley hugs Melrose (John Pankow). The film cuts to elevator doors opening and Brantley and Christy getting into the elevator.

What to Watch for and Ask Yourself

- What do these scenes suggest about the job seeking process?
- What do these scenes suggest about career management?
- Did Brantly behave ethically during his job interviews?

Concepts or Examples

☐ Job seeking

☐ Job interviewing skills

☐ Self-presentation

☐ Career management

☐ Impression management

☐ Alliances

Analysis

_____

_____

_____

_____

_____

_____

Personal Reactions

_____

_____

_____

_____

_____

_____

The Apartment

Black & White, 1960
Running Time: 2 hours, 6 minutes
Rating: NR
Distributor: *MGM/UA Home Video*

In this charming comedy, a lowly clerk moves up in an insurance company when he lets its executives use his apartment for their extramarital affairs. All does not go well when the company's president, J. D. Sheldrake (Fred MacMurray), uses the apartment—and his date, Fran Kubelik (Shirley MacLaine), tries to commit suicide. The clerk, C. C. Baxter (Jack Lemmon), helps bring her back to health and falls in love with her.

Scenes (Start: 1:53:45 — Stop: 2:01:58 — 8 minutes)

These scenes start with the black screen after Fran Kubelik's brother-in-law Karl (Johnny Seven) punches Baxter in the face. It opens with Baxter walking through the office wearing dark glasses and a dark overcoat. They end after Baxter enters the elevator and puts his hat on the janitor. The movie cuts to Baxter in his apartment.

What to Watch for and Ask Yourself

- Does Baxter face an ethical dilemma in these scenes?
- Should Baxter have said *yes* to Sheldrake's request to use his apartment and preserved his career advancement?
- Do you think such events could happen in organizations today?

Concepts or Examples

☐ Career

☐ Career management

☐ Power

☐ Political behavior

☐ Negotiation

☐ Ethical dilemma

Analysis

_____

_____

_____

_____

_____

_____

Personal Reactions

_____

_____

_____

_____

_____

References

Fisher, C. D., L. F. Schoenfeldt, and J. B. Shaw. 1995. *Human Resource Management*. Boston: Houghton Mifflin Company.

Mathis, R. and J. Jackson. 2000. *Human Resource Management*. Cincinnati: South-Western College Publishing.

CHAPTER 12

Human Resource Management: Selection

Selection is a crucial part of the human resource management process and it receives special attention in this chapter, which continues the discussion that began in Chapter 11 (Fisher, Schoenfeldt, and Shaw 1995; Mathis and Jackson 2000). Scenes from the following films show many ways to think about how important selection is as a function of human resource management:

- Butch Cassidy and the Sundance Kid
- Men in Black
- Crimson Tide
- Up Close & Personal

Butch Cassidy and the Sundance Kid contrasts selection procedures that yield different results. The sequence from *Men in Black* shows variations in selection criteria. *Crimson Tide* emphasizes the role of nonorganizational criteria in selection. *Up Close & Personal* shows different aspects of a job interview, especially its informality.

Butch Cassidy and the Sundance Kid (II)

Color, 1969
Running Time: 1 hour, 12 minutes
Rating: PG
Distributor: *Fox Video*

Director George Roy Hill's seriocomedy of a Western is as much a study of and a social commentary on the twilight of that American myth known as the Old West. For additional descriptions of this film and other scenes under discussion, see pages 84 and 244.

Scenes

The first set of scenes shows the selection of an employee. The second shows on-the-job performance. Stop after the first set of scenes and predict the job performance of Butch and Sundance on their first day as payroll guards. Then view the second set of scenes.*

1. (Start: 1:24:10 — Stop: 1:27:17 — 3 minutes)

These scenes start with shots of Butch Cassidy (Paul Newman), The Sundance Kid (Robert Redford), and Etta Place (Katherine Ross) dining in a restaurant celebrating their successful bank robbery. Butch sees a man in a straw hat. It is Sheriff LaForce (no name in credits) the leader of the posse. Butch and Sundance discuss going straight. These scenes end after mine owner Percy Garris (Strother Martin) walks away after hiring them as payroll guards.

2. (Start: 1:27:16 — Stop: 1:36:00 — 9 minutes)

The second set of scenes start with Butch and Sundance riding with Garris to get the payroll. They end after Sundance says, "Well, we've gone straight. What do we try now." The camera pans across the dead bandits. The film cuts to Etta, Butch, and Sundance talking about going straight.

What to Watch for and Ask Yourself

- Does mine owner Percy Garris use the right selection criteria?
- Does he change the selection process? If so, in what way?
- Will his hiring decision prove effective in protecting his payroll?

---

* Professor Robert Eder, Portland State University, recommended these scenes—J.E.C.

Concepts or Examples

☐ Selection process   ☐ Selection and performance

☐ Selection criteria   ☐ Selection criteria validity

Analysis

_____

_____

_____

_____

_____

_____

Personal Reactions

_____

_____

_____

_____

_____

_____

Men in Black

Color, 1997
Running Time: 1 hour, 38 minutes
Rating: PG-13
Distributor: *Columbia TriStar Home Video*

This box office smash film pairs the deadpan Tommy Lee Jones and the hip-hop singer and actor Will Smith as agents of MIB Special Services, an agency that monitors and polices aliens on the planet Earth. The special effects, including those in the selected scenes, often steal the show—as does Vincent D. Onofrio's performance as an intergalactic cockroach disguised in a human's skin. Unlike *Mars Attacks!*, which is a send-up of the traditional science fiction genre, this film is as much a social commentary on the beliefs of the UFO subculture as it is great comedy.*

Scenes (Start: 0:28:54 — Stop: 0:57:14 — 28 minutes)

These scenes start as J (Will Smith) looks up at a building inscription that reads, "Brooklyn Battery Tunnel. Triborough Bridge & Tunnel Authority." He enters the building. They end after J dresses in the black suit and puts on the sunglasses. He says to K (Tommy Lee Jones), "You know what the difference is between you and me? I make this look good." The film cuts to a storefront shot of G. Rosenberg Inc., Fine Jewelers. These scenes include selection, hiring, and the first day on the job.

What to Watch for and Ask Yourself

- What selection criteria did MIB Special Services use?
- Did they use both a testing and behavioral approach to selection?
- What core values did J learn on his first day on the job?

---

*My student, Siviengxay Limary, engineering graduate student, The University of New Mexico, originally recommended these scenes. — J.E.C.

Concepts or Examples

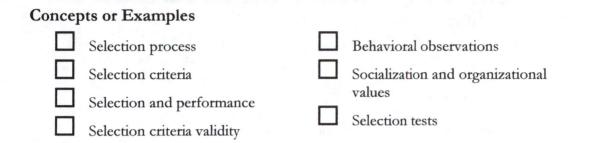

- ☐ Selection process
- ☐ Selection criteria
- ☐ Selection and performance
- ☐ Selection criteria validity

- ☐ Behavioral observations
- ☐ Socialization and organizational values
- ☐ Selection tests

Analysis

_____

_____

_____

_____

_____

Personal Reactions

_____

_____

_____

_____

_____

Crimson Tide

Color, 1995
Running Time: 1 hour, 56 minutes
Rating: R
Distributor: *Hollywood Pictures Home Video*

The Caine Mutiny meets *The Hunt for Red October* in this post-cold war military drama. The *U.S.S. Alabama*, a nuclear submarine, has set to sea with a new first officer. Events in Russia push that country and the United States to the brink of war. This tense situation causes Captain Ramsey (Gene Hackman) to become too mentally unstable to make the fateful decision to launch the *Alabama's* nuclear missiles.

Scenes (Start: 0:09:53 — Stop: 0:12:05 — 2 minutes)

These scenes start with a shot of Captain Ramsey's dog lying on a pillow. The title screen reads, "Directed by Tony Scott." They end after Ramsey says, "Welcome aboard the Alabama, son. Do me proud." Chief of the Boat Cob (George Dzundza) says, "Welcome aboard Mr. Hunter (Denzel Washington)." The movie cuts to a television newscast that some officers are watching in the briefing room.

What to Watch for and Ask Yourself

- What selection criteria did Captain Ramsey use to choose Lieutenant Commander Hunter?
- Did he use any non-job-related selection criteria?
- Do you expect Hunter to perform as expected? Why or why not?

Concepts or Examples

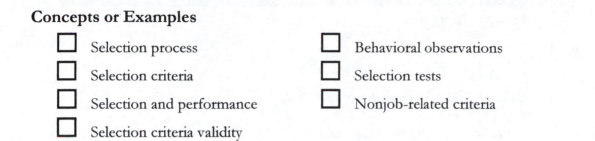

- ☐ Selection process
- ☐ Selection criteria
- ☐ Selection and performance
- ☐ Selection criteria validity

- ☐ Behavioral observations
- ☐ Selection tests
- ☐ Nonjob-related criteria

Analysis

_____

_____

_____

_____

_____

Personal Reactions

_____

_____

_____

_____

_____

Up Close & Personal

Color, 1996
Running Time: 2 hours, 4 minutes
Rating: PG-13
Distributor: *Touchstone Home Video*

Ambitious Tally Atwater (Michelle Pfeiffer) wants to break into television news reporting. She gets her chance when veteran television news reporter Warren Justice (Robert Redford) hires her at a Miami station. Romance follows, making their relationship complex and at times tumultuous. This well-acted film, based on a screenplay by novelists Joan Didion and John Gregory Dunne, has a lot of comedy—and a sad ending (Champoux 1999).

Scenes (Start: 0:05:47 — Stop: 0:12:26 — 7 minutes)

These scenes start with a panning shot of a satellite dish and the Channel 9 building. They end as Tally stares at Warren from the coffee machine. The film cuts to an outside shot of Channel 9 and pans to Tally talking on the telephone in the newsroom.

What to Watch for and Ask Yourself

- Did Warren Justice have explicit selection criteria for assessing Tally's abilities?
- Did he set clear performance expectations for Tally?
- Do you expect her to perform as desired by Justice? Why or why not?

Concepts or Examples

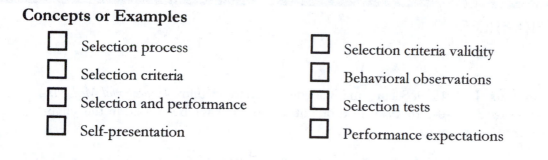

☐ Selection process   ☐ Selection criteria validity

☐ Selection criteria   ☐ Behavioral observations

☐ Selection and performance   ☐ Selection tests

☐ Self-presentation   ☐ Performance expectations

Analysis

_____

_____

_____

_____

_____

Personal Reactions

_____

_____

_____

_____

_____

References

Champoux, J. E. 1999. Seeing and Valuing Diversity in Film. *Educational Media International* 36: 310–316. *Note*: Portions of this article have been used in this chapter with permission.

Fisher, C. D., L. F. Schoenfeldt, and J. B. Shaw. 1995. *Human Resource Management.* Boston: Houghton Mifflin Company.

Mathis, R. L. and J. H. Jackson. 2000. *Human Resource Management with BNA Employment Guide.* Cincinnati: South-Western College Publishing.

CHAPTER 13

Labor–Management Relations

Labor–management relations refers to the quality of the relationship between an organization's management and nonmanagement employees (Fisher, Schoenfeldt, and Shaw 1995; Mathis and Jackson 2000). That relationship is negotiated when nonmanagement employees are union members or unilaterally set by the organization when there is no union. Employment issues that are the focus of labor–management relations include employment conditions, hours, wages, and benefits.

Organized labor in the United States has had a turbulent history since the late 1700s. The earliest craft unions were viewed as illegal conspiracies with no rights to exist. Federal legislation that emerged through the 1940s defined labor–management relations and specified the issues that could be settled by collective bargaining— the negotiation process used by labor and management to settle the terms of working conditions, hours, and compensation issues.

The following films have four scenes that show different aspects of labor–management relations and note some parts of its history in the United States:

- Matewan
- Norma Rae (I) & (II)
- Hoffa

Matewan (pronounced Mat'wan) has a powerful scene that shows some early efforts to form a union in a West Virginia coal mine. The two scenes from *Norma Rae* show a union organizer's frustration with company management and the final results of the organizing effort. *Hoffa* chronicles the life of a major American union leader. The selected scenes show parts of the negotiation process and the violence that often characterized the early labor movement.

Matewan

Color, 1987
Running Time: 2 hours, 10 minutes
Rating: R
Distributor: *Lorimar Home Video*

A gripping dramatization of the famous 1920s' Matewan massacre. West Virginia coal miners from diverse backgrounds (white, black, and immigrant) rally behind a union organizer. Terrible working conditions and oppressive management motivate them to risk the dangers of organizing. As in his other period film *Eight Men Out*, Director John Sayles has given this film a dialogue that is both historically accurate and colorful given the rich American slang of the time.

Scene (Start: 0:20:33 — Stop: 0:26:35 — 6 minutes)

This scene opens with Few Clothes Johnson (James Earl Jones) walking down a street at night. He tips his hat to the police chief (David Straithairn). The scene ends after the union meeting with Joe Kenehan (Chris Cooper) saying, "That's what a union is fellas. You better get used to it." The movie cuts to the church meeting with Danny Radnor (Will Oldham) preaching. The dialogue in this scene uses racial and ethnic terms that some presentday viewers might find offensive, but were common words in the 1920s.

What to Watch for and Ask Yourself

- How would you characterize labor–management relations in this 1920s West Virginia mining town?
- Were there strong underlying racial tensions among the mineworkers?
- Do you expect the desire to form a union to bond these men together, despite their differences?

Concepts or Examples

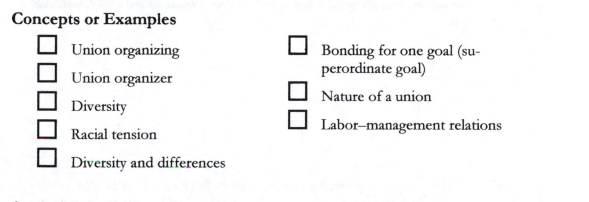

- ☐ Union organizing
- ☐ Union organizer
- ☐ Diversity
- ☐ Racial tension
- ☐ Diversity and differences

- ☐ Bonding for one goal (superordinate goal)
- ☐ Nature of a union
- ☐ Labor–management relations

Analysis

_____

_____

_____

_____

_____

_____

Personal Reactions

_____

_____

_____

_____

_____

Norma Rae (I)

Color, 1979
Running Time: 1 hour, 54 minutes
Rating: PG
Distributor: *CBS Fox Video*

Based on a true story, this powerful drama depicts the struggle of Southern textile workers in forming the first union in their textile mill. Reuben (Ron Leibman), a New York City labor organizer, builds Norma Rae's (Sally Field) confidence in herself and convinces her into leading her fellow workers to unionize. Field received an Academy Award for her performance. Another scene from this film is discussed on page 126 of this chapter—and on page 176 in Chapter 18.

Scenes (Start: 0:46:14 — Stop: 0:56:15 — 10 minutes)

These scenes begin with a shot of Norma Rae holding a Textile Workers Union of America (TWUA) flyer announcing a union organizing meeting that evening. The scenes follow her wedding. They end as the managers move the stock blocking the bulletin board and the shot of a pensive Norma Rae. The film cuts to Norma Rae crossing a motel parking lot.

What to Watch for and Ask Yourself

- What motivates these workers to form a union?
- Does management accept the workers' legal right to organize?
- What are the working conditions of these workers?

Concepts or Examples

☐ Union

☐ Union–management relations

☐ Poor working conditions

☐ Motivation to organize

☐ Oppressive supervision

☐ People as machines

☐ Hostile management

☐ Management interference with organizing effort

☐ Illegal interference

Analysis

_____

_____

_____

_____

_____

Personal Reactions

_____

_____

_____

_____

_____

_____

Norma Rae (II)

Color, 1979
Running Time: 1 hour, 54 minutes
Rating: PG
Distributor: *CBS Fox Video*

See page 124 of this chapter for a description of this film. Another scene is discussed on page 176 of Chapter 18.

Scenes (Start: 1:47:32 — Stop: 1:51:20 — 4 minutes)

These scenes begin with a shot of two workers tallying the union vote ballots. They end as the managers leave the area followed by the press and the workers cheer their victory. The movie cuts to an outside shot of Reuben (Ron Leibman) and Norma Rae (Sally Field).

What to Watch for and Ask Yourself

- What is your reaction to the workers' elation at winning the union election?
- Were they right or wrong in voting for the union?
- What do you believe was the nature of union–management relations before the vote? Were they good or bad?

Concepts or Examples

☐ Union ☐ Attitudes toward unions

☐ Union–management relations ☐ Attitudes toward management

☐ Reactions to unions

Analysis

_____

_____

_____

_____

_____

Personal Reactions

_____

_____

_____

_____

_____

Hoffa

Color, 1992
Running Time: 2 hours, 20 minutes
Rating: R
Distributor: *20th Century Fox Home Entertainment*

This powerfully acted film charts the rise and fall of powerful union leader, Jimmy Hoffa (Jack Nicholson). From almost nothing during the Great Depression, Hoffa helped build the Teamsters, a union with 2 million members by the late 1960s (Sheridan 1972). The film vividly portrays management's anti-labor sentiments of the period and the violence that was part of early labor organizing. Of special interest is Hoffa's personal—and mutual—animosity for Senator Robert F. Kennedy, a member of the senate subcommittee that investigated Hoffa in 1967 for corruption. This investigation opened the way for his successful prosecution and removal as Teamsters president. The film also speculates how Hoffa was murdered and disappeared without a trace in 1975.

Scenes (Start: 0:38:08 — Stop: 0:52:36 — 14 minutes)

These scenes start with Hoffa at a negotiating table saying, "Now wait a minute. I am a man with a legitimate grievance and a legitimate position." The scene fades in from an early roadhouse scene, after Bobby Ciaro (Danny DeVito) throws a cigarette to the floor and presses it under his shoe. These scenes end as the curtains close and the film fades to a wake for several dead Teamsters. The scenes have strong R-rated language.

What to Watch for and Ask Yourself

- Did organized labor at that time have the right to collectively bargain as asserted by Hoffa? Why or why not?
- Did the Railway Transport Agency management try to block Hoffa's organizing effort? Is *yes*, is such a blocking effort legal today?
- Were the Teamsters' members responding to Hoffa as a leader?

Concepts or Examples

- ☐ Labor–management relations
- ☐ Collective bargaining
- ☐ Negotiation
- ☐ Leadership
- ☐ Labor violence
- ☐ Picket line
- ☐ Labor history
- ☐ Union organizing effort

Analysis

_____

_____

_____

_____

_____

Personal Reactions

_____

_____

_____

_____

_____

References

Fisher, C. D., L. F. Schoenfeldt, and J. B. Shaw. 1995. *Human Resource Management.* Boston: Houghton Mifflin Company.

Mathis, R. L. and J. H. Jackson. 2000. *Human Resource Management with BNA Employment Guide.* Cincinnati: South-Western College Publishing.

Sheridan, W. 1972. *The Fall and Rise of Jimmy Hoffa.* New York: Saturday Review Press.

CHAPTER 14

Control

Control is a management process that monitors actual activities to ensure conformity to planned activities (Mockler 1984; Stoner and Freeman 1992, Chapter 20). Control also shows whether organizing and leading activities are getting intended results. The goal of control is to ensure the effective and efficient use of organizational resources in reaching its goal. Control processes typically have five elements:

1. Develop performance standards and performance measurement methods.
2. Measure performance of organizational processes.
3. Compare performance to standards.
4. Do nothing if performance complies with standards.
5. Take corrective action if performance does not meet standards.

Performance standards state measurable goals, how to reach those goals, and deadlines for reaching goals. **Performance measurement** can be continuous, as in monitoring aircraft landings, or periodic, as in assessing market share. **Corrective action** includes changing standards that are not right or changing organizational processes to more effectively meet the standard.

Scenes from the following films show different aspects of organizational control processes:

- Casino
- Broadcast News
- Pushing Tin
- Ground Control

The *Casino* scene shows the symbolic meaning of control. *Broadcast News* shows tight control and complex coordination at a television network. *Pushing Tin* uses complex high-technology control systems to guide airplane landings at a busy airport. *Ground Control* continues the air control theme without high technology.

Casino

Color, 1995
Running Time: 2 hours, 59 minutes
Rating: R
Distributor: *MCA Universal Home Video*

Martin Scorcese's lengthy, complex, and beautifully photographed study of 1970s' Las Vegas gambling casinos and their organized crime connections completes his trilogy that includes *Mean Streets* and *Goodfellas*. Ambition, greed, drugs, and sex ultimately destroy the mob's gambling empire. The film includes strong performances by Robert De Niro, Joe Pesci, and Sharon Stone. The violence and expletive-filled dialogue give *Casino* an R rating.

Scenes (Tape 1: Start: 0:24:22 — Stop: 0:26:09 — 2 minutes)

These scenes start with a close-up shot of Sam Rothstein (Robert De Niro) standing between two casino managers. His voice-over says, "In Vegas, everybody's gotta watch everybody else." They follow the scenes of deceiving the Japanese gambler. The scenes end with Sam and Billy Sugar (Don Rickles) watching the security monitor. The film cuts to the casino floor and focuses on Ginger's (Sharon Stone) winning.

What to Watch for and Ask Yourself

- What pattern of control do these scenes portray?
- What are the elements of the control system?
- What type of performance measurement do these scenes show: periodic or continuous?

Concepts or Examples

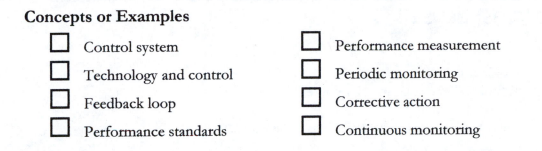

☐ Control system

☐ Technology and control

☐ Feedback loop

☐ Performance standards

☐ Performance measurement

☐ Periodic monitoring

☐ Corrective action

☐ Continuous monitoring

Analysis

_____

_____

_____

_____

_____

Personal Reactions

_____

_____

_____

_____

_____

Broadcast News (I)

Color, 1987
Running Time: 2 hours, 12 minutes
Rating: R
Distributor: *20th Century Fox Home Entertainment*

A romantic comedy featuring three well-defined and sharply different personalities. The opening scenes show their early personality development within their families.

Each character has distinctly different personality characteristics. Jane Craig (Holly Hunter), a bright, driven, compulsive news producer; Tom Grunich (William Hurt), a smooth, modern news anchor; and Aaron Altman (Albert Brooks), a veteran reporter who reacts jealously to Tom's on-camera success. The romantic triangle among these characters adds a strong comedic flavor to the film. For other scenes and descriptions of this film, see pages 202 and 264.

Scenes (Start: 0:47:45 — Stop: 0:55:52 — 8 minutes)

These scenes start in the broadcast control room. A person says, "Stand by for animation." They follow a scene of Aaron drinking away his sorrows in his apartment. They end as Tom leaves the control room saying, "Where's Jane. I'm still juiced."

What to Watch for and Ask Yourself

- What are the characteristics of this control process?
- Are there clear performance standards for a television broadcast?
- What is the feedback loop in this control process?

Concepts or Examples

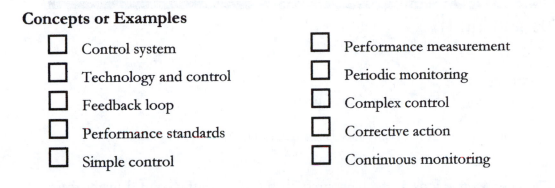

- ☐ Control system
- ☐ Technology and control
- ☐ Feedback loop
- ☐ Performance standards
- ☐ Simple control
- ☐ Performance measurement
- ☐ Periodic monitoring
- ☐ Complex control
- ☐ Corrective action
- ☐ Continuous monitoring

Analysis

_____

_____

_____

_____

_____

Personal Reactions

_____

_____

_____

_____

_____

Pushing Tin (I)

Color, 1999
Running Time: 2 hours, 4 minutes
Rating: R
Distributor: *20th Century Fox Home Entertainment*

This seriocomic look at the high stress world of air traffic control might scare some viewers away from flying. Top controller Nick Falzone (John Cusack) meets his equal after newcomer Russell Bell (Billy Bob Thornton) arrives. Competition between them brings dysfunctions to the operation. The complexity and stress of air traffic control operations clearly comes through. Another scene from *Pushing Tin* is discussed on page 152.

Scenes (Start: 0:12:35 — Stop: 0:16:58 — 4 minutes)

These scenes follow the title screen, "Fox 2000 Pictures and Regency Enterprises present." They open with shots of airplanes taxiing. These are the first scenes showing the air traffic controllers working with their consoles to control landings. They end after Nick Falzone gets up from his console and says, "I've go them lined up like Rockettes."

What to Watch for and Ask Yourself

- Which part of the operations management process does this control system affect?
- Do the controllers and pilots interact and give feedback to each other during the control process?
- Does this control system feature high or low stress?

Concepts or Examples

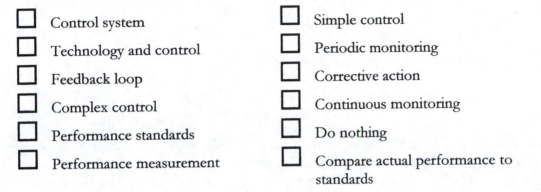

☐ Control system

☐ Technology and control

☐ Feedback loop

☐ Complex control

☐ Performance standards

☐ Performance measurement

☐ Simple control

☐ Periodic monitoring

☐ Corrective action

☐ Continuous monitoring

☐ Do nothing

☐ Compare actual performance to standards

Analysis

_____

_____

_____

_____

_____

_____

Personal Reactions

_____

_____

_____

_____

_____

_____

Ground Control

Color, 1998
Running Time: 1 hour, 37 minutes
Rating: PG-13
Distributor: *Trimark Home Video*

Jack Harris (Kiefer Sutherland) retired as an FAA controller after the crash of one of his planes in Chicago. Years later, his friend T. C. Bryant (Bruce McGill), asks Harris to help at the Phoenix center on an especially busy night. The night seems to end uneventfully when they have successfully landed all traffic. Events change dramatically when Trans Gulf Flight 47 suddenly shows up with no flight controls, no radio, and no instrument landing system.

Scenes (Start: 1:12:11 — Stop: 1:31:29 — 19 minutes)

These scenes start after the controllers have toasted their successful handling of unusually heavy traffic. Susan (Kellie McGillis), the center director, looks at the radar screens and says, "Beautiful sight." The film cuts to flight TEG47 with flight attendant Connie (Wendi Westbrook) asking the cockpit crew whether they were hungry. These scenes end after the pilot (Drew Snyder) tells the copilot (Steven Sax) to never tell his wife about what happened. The film cuts to an outside shot and passengers disembarking.

What to Watch for and Ask Yourself

- What are the elements of the control system that Jack Harris used?
- What is the feedback loop in this control system?
- Does this control system feature periodic or continuous monitoring?

Concepts or Examples

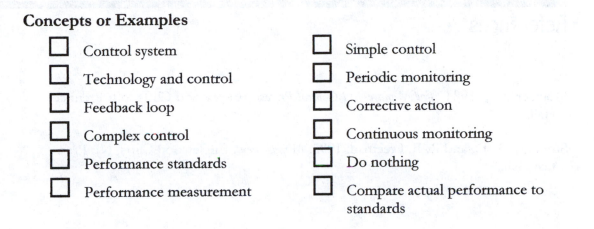

- ☐ Control system
- ☐ Technology and control
- ☐ Feedback loop
- ☐ Complex control
- ☐ Performance standards
- ☐ Performance measurement
- ☐ Simple control
- ☐ Periodic monitoring
- ☐ Corrective action
- ☐ Continuous monitoring
- ☐ Do nothing
- ☐ Compare actual performance to standards

Analysis

_____

_____

_____

_____

_____

Personal Reactions

_____

_____

_____

_____

_____

References

Mockler, R. J. 1984. *The Management Control Process.* Englewood Cliffs, NJ: Prentice Hall.

Stoner, J. A. F., and R. E. Freeman. 1992. *Management.* Englewood Cliffs, NJ: Prentice Hall.

Operations Management

Operations management includes the planning, organizing, direction, and controlling of an organization's processes that transform its inputs into its outputs (Render and Heizer 1998; Stoner and Freeman 1992, Ch. 21). **Inputs** include labor, raw materials, capital, and technology. **Outputs** are the organization's products and services. For example, Sony combines labor, raw materials, and technology to produce its DVD players. America Online combines technology and labor to provide its online services. Operations management has a feedback link between outputs and inputs that controls the efficiency and effectiveness of its operations (see Chapter 14).

Production and service organizations have different types of operations processes. **Production organizations** produce tangible and uniform products for later consumption—and with little direct customer participation. Sophisticated measurement systems compare output to previously set standards and specifications.

Service organizations produce intangibles that consumers immediately use. Operations are labor intensive with customer participation an essential element. Performance measurement usually is less sophisticated than in production organizations. A barber cuts hair to a visual standard, for example, not as measured by a laser measurement system.

These films offer scenes showing different aspects of operations management:

- Gung Ho
- A Bug's Life
- Wall Street
- Fawlty Towers: Gourmet Night

Gung Ho shows several aspects of operations management. A charming animated scene from *A Bug's Life* symbolically portrays operations management. *Wall Street* shows the complexity and stress of operations management in a stock brokerage firm. The "Waldorf Salad" episode of *Fawlty Towers* shows a dysfunctional operations management system.

Gung Ho (I)

Color, 1986
Running Time: 1 hour, 51 minutes
Rating: PG-13
Distributor: *Paramount Home Video*

Hunt Stevenson (Michael Keaton) goes to Japan to persuade Assan Motors to take over a closed automobile plant.* Once a major Hadleyville employer, the closed plant has brought economic depression to this small town. Culture clashes abound as Assan tries to bring Japanese management methods to Hadleyville's unionized employees. Stevenson, an employee liaison, tries to smooth relationships between the opposing groups, but does not always succeed. See page 290 for another discussion and description of this film.

Scenes (Start: 1:33:18 — Stop: 1:39:15 — 6 minutes)

These scenes start after Hunt and Kazihiro (Gedde Watanabe) talk by the river about having another chance to make the quota. Assan Motors has decided to close the Hadleyville plant. The two of them arrive in the plant parking lot to go to work. These scenes end with Hunt dancing jubilantly. The film cuts to a shot of Mr. Sakimoto's (Soh Yamamura) limousine arriving.

What to Watch for and Ask Yourself

- What type of operations management do these scenes show?
- Is there direct customer participation in these operations?
- Was there any example of warehousing the cars in these scenes?

---

*First recommended by Christopher J. van Lone, a former student at The Robert O. Anderson School of Management, The University of New Mexico. — J.E.C.

Concepts or Examples

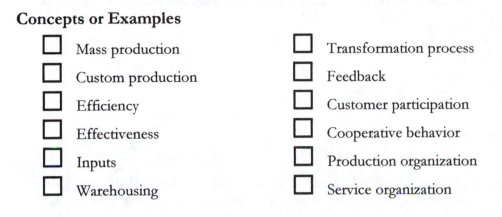

☐ Mass production
☐ Custom production
☐ Efficiency
☐ Effectiveness
☐ Inputs
☐ Warehousing

☐ Transformation process
☐ Feedback
☐ Customer participation
☐ Cooperative behavior
☐ Production organization
☐ Service organization

Analysis

_____

_____

_____

_____

_____

Personal Reactions

_____

_____

_____

_____

_____

A Bug's Life

Color, 1998
Running Time: 1 hour, 35 minutes
Rating: G
Distributor: *Walt Disney Home Video*

A group of freeloading grasshoppers dominate an ant colony. Hopper (Kevin Spacey), the grasshoppers' leader, perceives ants as an inferior species that serve grasshoppers. The otherwise conformist colony includes Flik (Dave Foley), a nonconforming—and innovative—ant. He tries to defend the colony with a group of "warrior" bugs he recruits in the city. These bugs are really laid-off flea circus performers, a fact unknown to Flik. Introducing the heterogeneous bugs to the ant colony leads to mayhem, humor, and finally, success (Champoux, 1999).

Scenes (Start: 1:00:33 — Stop: 1:06:05 — 6 minutes)

These scenes start after Flik has learned from Princess Atta (Julia Louis-Dreyfus) that Hopper is afraid of birds. He bursts out from behind two leaves saying, "Hopper's afraid of birds!" They end after they store the finished bird in a tree. Flik says, "Yes!" The movie pans from Flik to the offering rock with Mexican music starting in the background.

What to Watch for and Ask Yourself

- What type of transformation process do these scenes show?
- What inputs did they combine to make the bird?
- Did the differences between the ant colony members and the flea circus members reduce their effectiveness? Why or why not?

Concepts or Examples

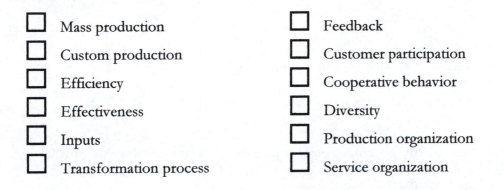

- ☐ Mass production
- ☐ Custom production
- ☐ Efficiency
- ☐ Effectiveness
- ☐ Inputs
- ☐ Transformation process

- ☐ Feedback
- ☐ Customer participation
- ☐ Cooperative behavior
- ☐ Diversity
- ☐ Production organization
- ☐ Service organization

Analysis

_____

_____

_____

_____

_____

Personal Reactions

_____

_____

_____

_____

_____

Wall Street

Color, 1987
Running Time: 2 hours, 4 minutes
Rating: R
Distributor: *20th Century Fox Home Entertainment*

Buddy Fox (Charlie Sheen), a young ambitious stock broker wants to learn from the financial wizardry of appropriately reptilian-named Gordan Gekko (Michael Douglas). Buddy does not know the extent of unethical behavior that Gekko is capable of to close a deal. A fellow broker remarks in the selected scene that Gekko had an "ethics bypass" at birth. Buddy's eventual discovery of Gekko's evil brings this Oliver Stone film to its predictable end.

Scenes (Start: 0:04:54 — Stop: 0:08:15 — 3 minutes)

These scenes follow the opening shots of Buddy Fox (Charlie Sheen) going to work at Jackson Steinem Co. They begin as the elevator doors open and Buddy and other workers get out. Carolyn (Tamara Tukie) the receptionist greets him. They end with the shot of the digital clock showing 03:50:22.

What to Watch for and Ask Yourself

- What are the elements of this operations management system?
- Does the customer participate in the system?
- What is the nature of feedback in this system? What responses appeared in the scenes?

Concepts or Examples

☐ Efficiency

☐ Effectiveness

☐ Inputs

☐ Transformation process

☐ Feedback

☐ Customer participation

☐ Cooperative behavior

☐ Diversity

☐ Production organization

☐ Service organization

Analysis

_____

_____

_____

_____

_____

Personal Reactions

_____

_____

_____

_____

_____

Fawlty Towers: Gourmet Night

Color, 1984
Running Time: 1 hour, 55 minutes
Rating: NR
Distributor: *20th Century Fox Home Entertainment*

This collection, culled from the best of BBC Television's *Fawlty Towers,* features the now classic "Waldorf Salad" episode. Other episodes on this tape include the title episode "Gourmet Night" and "The Kipper and the Corpse."

This British Broadcasting Company series showcases the sharp-tongued Basil Fawlty (John Cleese of Monty Python fame) and the more even tempered though lazy Sybil Fawlty (Prunella Scales). They operate Fawlty Towers, a hotel known for its bizarre permanent guests and a steady stream of temporary guests who always annoy Basil. Polly (Connie Booth) tries to add sensibility to the process. Manuel the waiter (Andrew Sachs) inserts his Spanish view as another source of disturbance.

Scenes (Start: 0:54:54 — Stop: 1:19:42 — 25 minutes)

The "Waldorf Salad" episode starts with Basil Fawlty and Mrs. Hamilton (Claire Nielson) at the front desk. Fawlty says, "Now. Ahem. If you would be so very kind as to fill that form out." Mr. Hamilton (Bruce Boa) arrives. These scenes end with Basil Fawlty trying to check in and a fade to the closing credits.

What to Watch for and Ask Yourself

- How efficient and effective is this operations management process?
- Does the client's presence in the process add to Basil Fawtly's disturbed reactions?
- Have the Fawlty's created a functional or dysfunctional operation? Why or why not?

Concepts or Examples

☐ Efficiency

☐ Effectiveness

☐ Inputs

☐ Transformation process

☐ Feedback

☐ Customer participation

☐ Functional operation

☐ Cooperative behavior

☐ Diversity

☐ Production organization

☐ Service organization

☐ Dysfunctional operation

Analysis

_____

_____

_____

_____

_____

_____

Personal Reactions

_____

_____

_____

_____

_____

_____

References

Champoux, J. E. 1999. Seeing and Valuing Diversity in Film. *Educational Media International* 36: 310–316. *Note:* Portions of this article have been used in this chapter with permission.

Render, B., and J. Heizer. 1998. *Operations Management.* Englewood Cliffs, NJ: Prentice Hall.

Stoner, J. A. F., and R. E. Freeman. 1992. *Management.* Englewood Cliffs, NJ: Prentice Hall.

CHAPTER 16

Information Systems

Information systems play a key role in helping managers keep an organization focused on its mission and goals (Kroenke 1992; Stoner and Freeman 1992, Ch. 22). The link between information systems and management control is tight. Without accurate, timely information, managers are unable to stay focused on their goals.

Information systems collect data from many sources and convert it to **information** that managers use to make decisions. **Data** are numbers and facts in raw form such as inventory levels, pricing, production output, and market share. **Information systems**, commonly called Management Information Systems or Decision Support Systems, process data and prepare reports for managers. These reports appear on computer terminals or in print form. The information system has transformed the raw data into systematic, understandable management information. Although most modern organizations use complex computer-based information systems, noncomputer systems, such as humans, can convert data to information and make decisions.

Scenes from the following four films show different aspects of information systems:

- Pushing Tin
- Analyze This
- Enemy of the State
- Star Trek: Generations

Pushing Tin shows how complex air traffic control systems help controllers safely land aircraft. *Analyze This* shows a human-based system that collects data and creates information. *Enemy of the State* portrays how National Security Agency personnel could access personal data and convert it to information for a management decision. *Star Trek: Next Generation* takes you to the 24th century and shows a highly advance information system helping Captain Picard's decision processes.

Pushing Tin (II)

Color, 1999
Running Time: 2 hours, 4 minutes
Rating: R
Distributor: *20th Century Fox Home Entertainment*

The macho world of flight controllers is exposed in this film in which the suspense feeds off the high level stress experienced by people in this profession. Though not quite a Merchant-Ivory production, it features Cate Blanchett of *Queen Elizabeth* and *The Talented Mr. Ripley* in her first Hollywood role as the wife of a flight controller. Another description of this film appears on page 136.

Scenes (Start: 0:37:34 — Stop: 0:41:32 — 4 minutes)

These scenes start with a panning shot across a highway near the Newark Airport. It shows many planes landing and taxiing. Russell Bell (Billy Bob Thornton) arrives in the control room carrying his folding chair. They end after Nick Falzone (John Cusack) says, "Nice talking to you Bell." He walks away. Then Bell replies, "Yeah, you too Nick."

What to Watch for and Ask Yourself

- What raw data and data sources does the flight control information system use?
- What forms of transformation were used to create information for the controllers?
- How did the Bell use the information to manage the landings?

Concepts or Examples

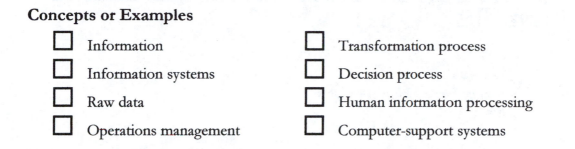

- ☐ Information
- ☐ Information systems
- ☐ Raw data
- ☐ Operations management

- ☐ Transformation process
- ☐ Decision process
- ☐ Human information processing
- ☐ Computer-support systems

Analysis

_____

_____

_____

_____

_____

Personal Reactions

_____

_____

_____

_____

_____

Analyze This

Color, 1999
Running Time: 1 hour, 44 minutes
Rating: R
Distributor: *Warner Home Video*

New York mob boss Paul Vitti (Robert De Niro) has lost his nerve and does not want his opponents to know. He has panic attacks. He has lost some of his sex drive with his mistress. Vitti seeks the help of psychiatrist Ben Sobel (Billy Crystal) who quickly begins to fear for his life. Excellent character portrayals by both actors create an engaging cinema experience.

Scenes (Start: 0:22:48 — Stop: 0:29:18 — 6 minutes)

These scenes, following Vitti's stay in the emergency room, start in Sobel's office with Carl (Neil Pepe) his patient. Sobel says, "Carl, I am detecting a pattern here. You seem to settle too easily for things." Carl says, "You're right, I do." The scenes end as Vitti pinches Sobel's cheek and says to Sobel, "You're good!" The film cuts to shots of a clothing factory and Primo Sindone (Chazz Palminteri) getting fitted for a suit.

What to Watch for and Ask Yourself

- What is Sobel's source of raw data. What are the data?
- How does Sobel process the data to create information for his diagnosis?
- Does the information create any changes that are similar to processes in organizations?

Concepts or Examples

- ☐ Raw data
- ☐ Information
- ☐ Information processing
- ☐ Data sources

- ☐ Role of training
- ☐ Decisions and change
- ☐ Operations systems

Analysis

_____

_____

_____

_____

_____

_____

Personal Reactions

_____

_____

_____

_____

_____

Enemy of the State

Color, 1998
Running Time: 2 hours, 12 minutes
Rating: R
Distributor: *Touchstone Home Video*

A nonstop thriller about Washington, DC lawyer Robert Clayton Dean's (Will Smith) unexpected clash with ruthless National Security Agency (NSA) head Reynolds (Jon Voight). Under Reynold's direction, NSA agents use advanced technology to destroy Dean's life. A disavowed-agent of the NSA, Brill (Gene Hackman), with some hesitation and reluctance, steps in to help Dean fight back against seemingly impossible odds.

Scenes (Start: 0:42:26 — Stop: 0:44:55 — 3 minutes)

These scenes start with an aide entering an NSA operations area carrying a file folder. Fiedler's (Jack Black) voice-over says, "We are running a comprehensive database search. Bryan (the aide) did a preliminary analysis and comparison and he came up with some pretty interesting stuff." The scenes follow the family scenes in the Dean home and after Carla Dean (Regina King) leaves with the children. They end with Reynolds looking at the computer screens saying, "Maybe its everything. Let's get it and find out." The film cuts to Dean sipping wine at home. These scenes have a brief shot of some scantily clad women in the lingerie shop.

What to Watch for and Ask Yourself

- What raw data and data sources did Fiedler and his fellow technicians use?
- What forms of transformation were used to create information?
- How did the information affect operations management and decision processes?

Concepts or Examples

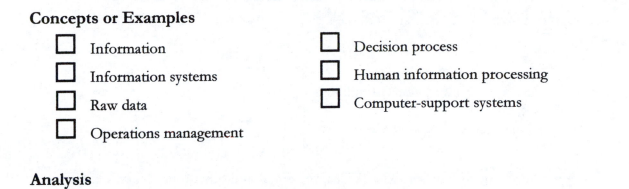

☐ Information

☐ Information systems

☐ Raw data

☐ Operations management

☐ Decision process

☐ Human information processing

☐ Computer-support systems

Analysis

_____

_____

_____

_____

_____

_____

Personal Reactions

_____

_____

_____

_____

_____

Star Trek: Generations (I)

Color, 1994
Running Time: 1 hour, 51 minutes
Rating: PG
Distributor: *Paramount Pictures Corp.*

Retired Captain James T. Kirk (William Shatner) and other retired Starfleet officers, Scotty (James Doohan) and Chekov (Walter Koenig), are guests aboard the *Enterprise-B*. The test flight of this newly christened starship presents several crises and decisions to people in leadership roles. The film also features Captain Jean-Luc Picard (Patrick Stewart) in a 24th-century adventure to stop the evil physicist Soran (Malcolm McDowell) from killing tens of millions of people. Scenes from this film are also discussed on page 178.

Scenes (Start: 0:57:06 — Stop: 1:03:01 — 6 minutes)

These scenes start with a space shot of the *Enterprise* and Captain's Picard's voice-over describing his log entry. They follow the interrogation of Geordi (LeVar Burton) by Soran on board a Klingon ship. Data (Brent Spiner) and Picard are going to work together in the stellar cartography room. Data has had an emotion chip embedded in his system. He now finds it difficult to manage and control his feelings. The scenes end as Picard calls the bridge and he and leaves with Data. The film cuts to a space shot of the *Enterprise*.

What to Watch for and Ask Yourself

- What is the raw data used by the stellar cartography system?
- What information is produced by the system?
- How does that information affect Captain Picard's decision process and the operation of the starship?

Concepts or Examples

- ☐ Raw data
- ☐ Information
- ☐ Data accuracy
- ☐ Decision process

- ☐ Data integration
- ☐ Operations management
- ☐ Data sources

Analysis

_____

_____

_____

_____

_____

_____

Personal Reactions

_____

_____

_____

_____

_____

References

Kroenke, D. M. 1992. *Management Information Systems*. New York: McGraw-Hill.

Stoner, J. A. F., and R. E. Freeman. 1992. *Management*. Englewood Cliffs, NJ: Prentice Hall.

Power and Political Behavior

Power and political behavior pervade organizational life. Each works with the other to affect people's behavior at all organizational levels.

Power is a person's ability to get something done the way the person wants it done (Salancik and Pfeffer 1977). It is the ability to affect other people's behavior and overcome resistance to changing direction. Power often is used to overcome opposition and get people to do what they otherwise might not do (Pfeffer 1992). It includes the ability to gather physical and human resources and put them to work to reach whatever goals the person wants to reach (Kanter 1977).

Political behavior in organizations focuses on getting, developing, and using power to reach a desired result in situations of uncertainty or conflict over choices. Such behavior often happens outside accepted channels of authority in an organization. You can view political behavior as unofficial, unsanctioned behavior to reach some goal (Griener and Schein 1988; Madison et al. 1980; Mintzberg 1983; Salancik and Pfeffer 1977). People use political behavior to affect decisions, get scarce resources, and earn the cooperation of people outside their direct authority. Behavior that uses power, builds power, or tries to influence others is political (Mayes and Allen 1977).

These films have scenes that show aspects of power and political behavior:

- Working Girl
- With Honors
- El Mariachi
- The Godfather

The closing scenes from *Working Girl* dramatically and humorously show the meaning of political behavior in organizations. *With Honors* effectively shows three separate power relationships and the different sources of power in each. *El Mariachi* shows different aspects of the sources of power, although with some violence. The scenes from *The Godfather* are dramatic, nonviolent portrayals of power and political behavior.

161

Working Girl

Color, 1988
Running Time: 1 hour, 55 minutes
Rating: R
Distributor: *20th Century Fox Home Entertainment*

Tess McGill (Melanie Griffith) continually tries to move from a secretary's position to a management position. She is not successful after several efforts. Her boss Katherine Parker (Sigourney Weaver) breaks her leg in a skiing accident, opening an opportunity for Tess to take over her job temporarily. Tess develops some good ideas for an acquisition by Trask Industries. Jack Trainer (Harrison Ford), an investment banker, helps Tess present the proposal but Katherine returns to take it as her own.

Scenes (Start: 1:39:07 — Stop: 1:47:14 — 8 minutes)

These scenes start with Tess McGill clearing her desk and saying goodbye to her coworkers. They follow the scenes of Tess on the ferry crossing to Manhattan. They end when she accepts the job offer from Mr. Trask—and she and Jack embrace. Her former coworkers applaud. The film cuts to Tess and Jack having breakfast before going to work.

What to Watch for and Ask Yourself

- What is Tess McGill's power base?
- Is Tess working within or outside her normal reporting relationships?
- Is there a shift of power within these scenes? Did anyone gain or lose power?

Concepts or Examples

☐ Power ☐ Political strategy

☐ Power dimensions ☐ Power dynamics

☐ Political behavior ☐ Power loss

Analysis

_____

_____

_____

_____

_____

_____

Personal Reactions

_____

_____

_____

_____

_____

With Honors

Color, 1994
Running Time: 1 hour, 40 minutes
Rating: PG-13
Distributor: *Warner Home Video*

Harvard senior, Monty Kessler (Brendon Fraser) loses the only copy of his thesis. It falls into the hands of street bum Simon Wilder (Joe Pesci). Simon is willing to return it, one page at a time, in exchange for favors such as food, clothing, and a place to live. Simon is feisty and perceives himself as no ordinary bum: "I'm a bum. But ... I'm a Harvard bum." He becomes entangled in the lives of Monty and his roommates. Monty and Simon develop a close relationship as the film unfolds.

Scenes (Start: 0:04:44 — Stop: 0:17:05 — 12 minutes)

These scenes start with the opening campus shot and the voice-over about the crush of being a Harvard senior. They follow the black open titling scenes. The scenes end when Monty leaves the building and meets Courtney (Moira Kelly). She says, "You didn't get it?" The movie cuts to the examination of donuts under a magnifying glass.

What to Watch for and Ask Yourself

- What are the bases of power in Simon's relationship with Monty?
- Which dimensions of power relationships do the scenes show?
- Does Simon behave ethically?

Concepts or Examples

☐ Power

☐ Sources of power

☐ Power relationships

☐ Dimensions of power relationships

Analysis

_____

_____

_____

_____

_____

Personal Reactions

_____

_____

_____

_____

_____

El Mariachi

Color, 1993
Spanish, with English subtitles
Running Time: 1 hour, 21 minutes
Rating: R
Distributor: *Columbia TriStar Home Video*

El Mariachi (Carlos Gallardo) wants to be a *mariachi* (traveling musician), as were his great-grandfather, grandfather, and father. His guitar case and black clothing cause him to be misidentified as Azul, an enemy of drug lord Moco.

The story about making this film is as enjoyable as the film (Connors and Craddock 2000, 293). Director Robert Rodriquez stayed in a research hospital to raise money to make the film. He and his crew of family, relatives, and cast shot the film in eleven consecutive days with no retakes and using borrowed equipment. The closing cast credits are among the most amusing to watch.

Scenes (Start: 0:00:49 — Stop: 0:07:44 — 7 minutes)

These scenes start the film beginning after the Columbia Pictures logo. They show a jeep and the *carcel publica* (public jail). A police van arrives. They end after the screen goes black followed by a text screen reading, "Columbia Pictures presents."

What to Watch for and Ask Yourself

- What are the bases of power for the jail guards?
- What are the bases of power for the prisoners?
- What are the bases of power for the gunmen?

Concepts or Examples

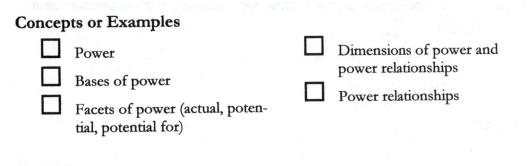

☐ Power

☐ Bases of power

☐ Facets of power (actual, potential, potential for)

☐ Dimensions of power and power relationships

☐ Power relationships

Analysis

_____

_____

_____

_____

_____

_____

Personal Reactions

_____

_____

_____

_____

_____

The Godfather (II)

Color, 1972
Running Time: 2 hours, 51 minutes
Rating: R
Distributor: *Paramount Pictures Corp.*

Nino Rota's music provides a sweeping score for this classic film about the Corleone crime family. Director Francis Ford Coppola and the novelist Mario Puzo won an Academy Award for best screenplay. For additional descriptions and scenes from this film, see pages 54 and 184.

Scenes (Tape 2. Start: 0:10:01 — Stop: 0:16:49 — 7 minutes)

Months of fighting among the families with the loss of many lives, including Don Corleone's son Santino (James Caan), precede these scenes. Michael Corleone (Al Pacino) is preparing to return to the United States from Sicily.

These scenes start with a shot of a building and the cut to Barzini (Richard Conte) with Don Corleone's (Marlon Brando) voice-over, "Don Barzini, I wanna thank you for help'n me organize this meeting here today." The scenes end as Frank Hagen (Robert Duvall) and Corleone are riding in a car. Coreleone says, "But I didn't know until this day that it was . . . Barzini all along." The film cuts to a scene of a school.

What to Watch for and Ask Yourself

- What are Don Corleone's sources of power?
- What are the sources of power of the other family heads?
- What facets of power appear in these scenes?

Concepts or Examples

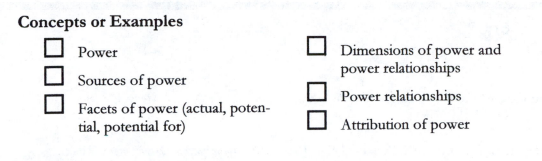

☐ Power

☐ Sources of power

☐ Facets of power (actual, potential, potential for)

☐ Dimensions of power and power relationships

☐ Power relationships

☐ Attribution of power

Analysis

_____

_____

_____

_____

_____

_____

Personal Reactions

_____

_____

_____

_____

_____

_____

References

Connors, M., and J. Craddock, eds. 2000. *VideoHound's Golden Movie Retriever*. Detroit: Visible Ink Press.

Griener, L. E., and V. E. Schein. 1988. *Power and Organization Development*. Reading, MA: Addison-Wesley.

Kanter, R. M. 1977. *Men and Women of the Corporation*. New York: Basic Books.

Madison, D. L., R. W. Allen, L. W. Porter, P. A. Renwick, and B. T. Mayes. 1980. Organizational Politics: An Exploration of Managers' Perceptions. *Human Relations* 33: 79–100.

Mayes, B. T., and R. W. Allen. 1977. Toward a Definition of Organizational Politics. *Academy of Management Journal* 2: 635–644.

Mintzberg, H. 1983. *Power In and Around Organizations*. Englewood Cliffs, NJ: Prentice Hall.

Pfeffer, J. 1992. *Managing with Power: Politics and Influence in Organizations*. Boston: Harvard Business School Press.

Salancik, G. R., and J. Pfeffer. 1977. Who Gets Power and How They Hold Onto It: A Strategic Contingency Model of Power. *Organizational Dynamics* 5: 3–21.

CHAPTER 18

Leadership and Management

Leadership is a process of social influence involving two or more people: the leader and a follower or a potential follower (Bass 1990; House and Aditya 1997; House and Baetz 1979; Nutt and Backoff 1997). The influence process has two dimensions. The first is the intention of the leader to affect the behavior of at least one other person. The second is the extent the target perceives the influence as acceptable. Perception and attribution are important elements of the leadership process. The person who is the target of the influence effort must attribute it to a specific person and consider it acceptable.

Leaders can hold formal organization positions or emerge spontaneously within an organization. The formal positions carry titles such as Manager, Supervisor, or Vice-President. Both the qualities of the position and the characteristics of the person holding it contribute to leadership. Other people play leadership roles, although they do not hold formally appointed positions. Such leaders are emergent leaders found within formal and informal groups in organizations.

There are differences between **managers** and **leaders**. Managers sustain and control organizations; leaders try to change them. Managers follow the present vision for the organization; they do not create a new one. Leaders have a vision of how an organization could be better and inspire followers to pursue that vision.

This chapter discusses leadership scenes from the following films:

- The American President
- City Hall
- Norma Rae
- Star Trek: Generations

The American President has an early scene that shows different leadership traits of the President and some key staff members. *City Hall* shows a leader expressing a vision in a potentially hostile environment. *Norma Rae* shows a woman in a leadership role. The opening scenes of *Star Trek: Generations* effectively show both the absence and presence of leadership.

The American President

Color, 1995
Running Time: 1 hour, 54 minutes
Rating: PG-13
Distributor: *Columbia TriStar Home Video*

President Andrew Shepherd (Michael Douglas), a widower, decides to romantically pursue a lobbyist (Annette Benning), but does not realistically assess the political implications. The portrayal of the President as witty, handsome, honest, and decisive will both fit and not fit the stereotypes currently held by Americans.

Scenes (Start: 0:12:17 — Stop: 0:17:42 — 3 minutes)

These scenes start with the shot of the White House just after the opening credits. They end after President Andrew Shepherd leaves the room. The movie cuts to a street shot.

What to Watch for and Ask Yourself

- Which leadership traits does the President show?
- Which leadership traits does the Chief of Staff A. J. MacInery (Martin Sheen) show?
- Which leadership traits does Lewis Rothschild (Michael J. Fox) show?

Concepts or Examples

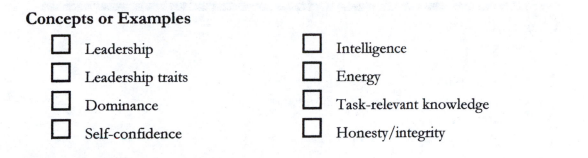

☐ Leadership   ☐ Intelligence

☐ Leadership traits   ☐ Energy

☐ Dominance   ☐ Task-relevant knowledge

☐ Self-confidence   ☐ Honesty/integrity

Analysis

_____

_____

_____

_____

_____

Personal Reactions

_____

_____

_____

_____

_____

City Hall

Color, 1996
Running Time: 1 hour, 52 minutes
Rating: R
Distributor: *Columbia TriStar Home Video*

Mayor John Pappas' (Al Pacino) administration is battered by the death of a Brooklyn six-year-old boy in a drug-related shoot-out. This film shows the deception, corruption, power relationships, and ambition that can lurk at all levels of city government. Pappas' challenge is to turn his administration in the right direction while pursuing his more lofty political ambitions.

Scene (Start: 0:43:01 — Stop: 0:49:07 — 6 minutes)

This scene opens with a shot of a church. Mayor Pappas is attending the funeral of the murdered boy. He wants to address the people attending the funeral but is not warmly welcomed. The scene ends as the camera pans to the flowers on the casket.

What to Watch for and Ask Yourself

- Is Mayor Pappas trying to describe a new vision or future for city?
- Is he believable?
- Do the people in the audience accept him as a leader who can bring needed change?

Concepts or Examples

☐ Vision

☐ Leadership

☐ Values

☐ Transformational leadership

☐ Charismatic leadership

☐ Leadership perceptions

Analysis

_____

_____

_____

_____

_____

Personal Reactions

_____

_____

_____

_____

_____

Norma Rae (III)

Color, 1979
Running Time: 1 hour, 57 minutes
Rating: PG
Distributor: *20th Century Fox Home Entertainment*

Sectioned See page 124 of Chapter 13 for a description of this film. Another scene is also discussed in that chapter on page 126.

Scene (Start: 1:31:00 — Stop: 1:37:56 — 8 minutes)

The scene begins with a shot of a door with a sign that says, "Transfer Traffic Only." Norma Rae opens the door and goes to the bulletin board to copy a memo. Mangement had prepared the memo saying the Black workers would try to dominate the union. The scene ends after the manager goes into his office and closes the door. The movie cuts to an outside shot of a police car.

What to Watch for and Ask Yourself

- Which leadership traits does Norma Rae have?
- Do the workers begin to perceive her as a leader?
- Which views of leadership does she portray?

Concepts or Examples

- ☐ Charisma
- ☐ Leadership behavior
- ☐ Leadership mystique
- ☐ Self-confidence
- ☐ Energy

Analysis

_____

_____

_____

_____

_____

_____

Personal Reactions

_____

_____

_____

_____

_____

_____

Star Trek: Generations (II)

Color, 1994
Running Time: 1 hour, 51 minutes
Rating: PG
Distributor: *Paramount Pictures Corp.*

Retired Captain James T. Kirk (William Shatner) and fellow retired Starfleet officers, Scotty (James Doohan) and Chekov (Walter Koenig), are guests aboard the *Enterprise-B* for its maiden voyage. The *Enterprise's* other skipper, Captain Jean-Luc Picard (Patrick Stewart), also stars in this space adventure that shows the leadership characteristics of different people in different situations. Another scene from this film is discussed on page 158.

Scenes (Start: 0:08:20 — Stop: 0:19:39 — 11 minutes)

These scenes start with a shot of the *Enterprise-B* docked in the spaceport. The screen reads, "Directed by David Carson." Shortly after leaving the spaceport, the crew learns of two ships in distress. Several crises erupt that test the leadership skills of those in command. The scenes end after Captain Kirk enters the elevator and the doors close.

What to Watch for and Ask Yourself

- What leadership traits do you ascribe to Captain Harriman (Alan Ruck)?
- What leadership traits do you ascribe to Captain Kirk?
- Which leadership theories best describe the behavior of the two captains?

Concepts or Examples

☐ Leadership

☐ Leadership traits

☐ Transformational leadership

☐ Charismatic leadership

☐ Leadership mystique

☐ Absence of leadership

Analysis

_____

_____

_____

_____

_____

_____

Personal Reactions

_____

_____

_____

_____

_____

References

Bass, B. M. 1990. *Bass & Stogdill's Handbook of Leadership: Theory, Research, & Managerial Applications.* New York: The Free Press.

House, R. J., and R. N. Aditya. 1997. The Social Scientific Study of Leadership: Quo Vadis? *Journal of Management* 23: 409–473.

House, R. J., and M. L. Baetz. 1979. Leadership: Some Empirical Generalizations and New Research Directions. In *Research in Organizational Behavior,* ed. B. M. Staw. Greenwich, CT: JAI Press, 341–423.

Nutt, P. C., and R. W. Backoff. 1997. Crafting Vision. *Journal of Management Inquiry* 6: 308-328.

Organizational Culture

Organizational culture is a complex and deep aspect of organizations that can strongly affect organization members (Alvesson and Berg 1992; Schein 1984; Schein 1992). **Organizational culture** includes the values, norms, rites, rituals, ceremonies, heroes, and scoundrels in an organization's history (Deal and Kennedy 1982). It defines the content of what a new employee needs to learn to be accepted as a member of the organization (Martin1992; Trice & Beyer 1993, Ch 1).

Organizational cultures divide into multiple **subcultures**. They grow readily within departments, divisions, and different operating locations of an organization.

People can view organizational culture at three different but related levels. **Artifacts** are the most visible parts of an organization's culture. They are the obvious features of an organization such as sounds, architecture, smells, behavior, attire, and language. **Values**, the next level of awareness, tell organization members what they "ought" to do in various situations. **Basic assumptions**, an almost invisible level of organization culture, are another form of values. Veteran organization members often are not consciously aware of basic assumptions.

Organizational culture concepts appear subtly in some films and boldly in others. The following films offer both possibilities.

- Top Gun
- The Godfather
- Dead Poets Society
- The Hunt for Red October

Top Gun boldly shows some more obvious aspects of organizational culture. The opening scenes of *The Godfather* show some subtle, often hidden, aspects of organizational culture. *Dead Poets Society* shows some obvious aspects of organizational culture in a nonmilitary setting. *The Hunt for Red October* has a short scene showing the role of stories in an organization's culture.

Top Gun

Color, 1986
Running Time: 1 hour, 40 minutes
Rating: PG
Distributor: *Paramount Pictures Corp.*

An action-based film that simply screams with aspects of naval aviation culture. Part of the film focuses on the relationships between Maverick (Tom Cruise) and a sultry civilian instructor (Kelly McGillis). The selected scenes show several aspects of naval aviation organizational culture. The use of real U.S. Navy people and equipment at various places gives a strong sense of reality.

Scenes (Start: 0:01:47 — Stop: 0:17:30 — 17 minutes)

These scenes begin with the Paramount logo and background music followed by the opening title credits. Closely watch the action behind them. The scenes behind the credits were shot on a U.S. Navy aircraft carrier using U.S. Navy people, not actors and actresses. The entire sequence ends after the commander wishes Maverick and Goose (Anthony Edwards) good luck.

What to Watch for and Ask Yourself

- What artifacts or physical characteristics of U.S. Naval aviation culture do the scenes show?
- Were any subcultures shown in the scenes? What defined the subcultures?
- What values do you infer from the scenes?

Concepts or Examples

- ☐ Dimensions of organizational culture
- ☐ Levels of organizational culture (artifacts, values, basic assumptions),
- ☐ Perspectives on organizational culture

- ☐ Cultural symbolism
- ☐ Functions of organizational culture
- ☐ Dysfunctions of organizational culture

Analysis

_____

_____

_____

_____

_____

Personal Reactions

_____

_____

_____

_____

_____

The Godfather (III)

Color, 1972
Running Time: 2 hours, 51 minutes
Rating: R
Distributor: *Paramount Pictures Corp.*

Another look at a powerful Italian-American family led by Don Corleone and its dynastic struggle with the five other Mafia families that control organized crime in America. *The Godfather* spawned two sequels and was selected in 1990 for inclusion in the Library of Congress' National Film Registry as one of its American films "Film Treasures." For additional descriptions and scenes from *The Godfather*, see pages 54 and 168.

Scene (Tape 1. Start: 0:01:25 — Stop: 0:07:38 — 6 minutes)

This scene starts after the opening titles with a man's voice-over: "I believe in America." The movie cuts to the face of the man speaking. The scene ends after Don Corleone (Marlon Brando) says to Tom Hagen (Robert Duvall), "I mean, we are not murder'n in spite of what this undertaker said." Don Corleone then sniffs his lapel flower. The film cuts to the wedding reception.

What to Watch for and Ask Yourself

- What levels of this organization's culture appear in this scene?
- Does this scene show any values that guide behavior in this culture?
- Is the culture functional or dysfunctional for this organization?

Concepts or Examples

☐ Organizational culture   ☐ Artifacts/physical characteristics

☐ Values   ☐ Espoused values

☐ Basic assumptions   ☐ In-use values

Analysis

_____

_____

_____

_____

_____

_____

Personal Reactions

_____

_____

_____

_____

_____

Dead Poets Society

Color, 1989
Running Time: 2 hours, 8 minutes
Rating: PG
Distributor: *Touchstone Home Video*

Charismatic English teacher, John Keating (Robin Williams), tries to unleash the creativity and individuality of his young New England preparatory school students. Their behavior is not always accepted by the staid administration. Keating is eventually fired because of the belief that he had too powerful an effect on student behavior.

Scene (Start: 0:00:53 — Stop: 0:04:44 — 4 minutes)

This scene starts after the title screen that reads, "A Steven Haft Production in association with Witt-Thomas Productions". It ends after the introduction of Mr. Keating. He sits down and the film cuts to an outside scene.

What to Watch for and Ask Yourself

- What are some physical artifacts of the school's organizational culture?
- What are some dominant values in its culture?
- What is the function of rites and rituals in this situation?

Concepts or Examples

☐ Organizational culture   ☐ Values

☐ Rites and rituals   ☐ Basic assumptions

☐ Physical artifacts

Analysis

_____

_____

_____

_____

_____

Personal Reactions

_____

_____

_____

_____

_____

The Hunt for Red October (II)

Color, 1990
Running Time: 2 hours, 15 minutes
Rating: PG
Distributor: *Paramount Pictures Corporation*

This film adaptation of Tom Clancy's novel about a high-tech, top-secret Soviet submarine is an intense undersea adventure. Another scene from this film is discussed on page 96. The all-star cast includes Sean Connery, Alec Baldwin, and James Earl Jones.

Scene (Start: 0:12:20 — Stop: 0:14:41 — 3 minutes)

The scene starts with a voice-over saying, "Do you hear it?" It follows a scene of a submerged submarine and titling that reads, "US Dallas Los Angeles Class Attack Sub 100 miles Northwest of Polijarny Inlet." The scene ends as Seaman Jones (Courtney B. Vance) takes the sonar alarm and says, "Conn. Sonar. New contact. Bearing zero, niner, seven. Designate contact number sierra 35." The movie cuts to the conning tower and a shot of the loudspeaker.

What to Watch for and Ask Yourself

- In what part of an organization's culture do stories reside?
- Does the story convey any organizational values?
- What role did the story play in this situation?

Concepts or Examples

☐ Values

☐ Basic assumptions

☐ Artifacts

☐ Socialization—training

☐ Accuracy

Analysis

_____

_____

_____

_____

_____

_____

Personal Reactions

_____

_____

_____

_____

_____

References

Alvesson, M., and P. O. Berg. 1992. *Corporate Culture and Organizational Symbolism.* New York: Hawthorne/Walter de Gruyter.

Deal, T. E., and A. A. Kennedy. 1982. *Corporate Cultures: The Rites and Rituals of Corporate Life.* Reading, MA: Addison-Wesley.

Martin, J. 1992. *Cultures in Organizations: Three Perspectives.* New York: Oxford University Press.

Schein, E. H. 1984. Coming to a New Awareness of Organizational Culture. *Sloan Management Review* 25: 3–16.

Schein, E. H. 1992. *Organizational Culture and Leadership.* San Francisco: Jossey-Bass.

Trice, H.. M., and J. M. Beyer. 1993. *The Cultures of Work Organizations.* Englewood Cliffs, NJ: Prentice Hall.

Organizational Socialization

Organizational socialization is a powerful process by which people learn the content of an organization's culture (Ott 1989; Schein 1992; Trice and Beyer 1993). It affects individual behavior and helps shape and maintain the organization's culture (Schein 1968; Van Maanen and Schein 1979). Organizational socialization happens in three stages. The product of one stage becomes the input to the next stage.

Choice: Anticipatory Socialization is the first stage of socialization a person experiences. This stage happens before a person joins an organization or takes a new job in the same organization. The anticipatory stage builds expectations about what it is like to work for the organization. The **Entry/Encounter** stage occurs after entering the organization. A new employee learns whether his or her expectations are consistent with the reality of organization life (Feldman 1976; Fisher 1986; Van Maanen and Schein 1979).

Change takes place during the encounter stage, as it flows and blends into the **Metamorphosis** stage. If a new employee has successfully resolved the demands from the multiple sources of socialization, he or she begins to feel comfortable in the new role (Feldman 1981; Van Manaan and Schein 1977).

The following films have scenes that give a range of portrayals of aspects of organizational socialization:

- The Firm
- The Hudsucker Proxy
- An Officer and a Gentleman
- Snow White and the Seven Dwarfs

The opening scenes from *The Firm* show the early stages of socialization. Scenes from *The Hudsucker Proxy* humorously show a new employee's first encounter with an organization. *An Officer and Gentleman* is more serious. It shows the transformation of a new recruit into a U.S. Naval officer. The transformation of the queen to a witch in *Snow White and the Seven Dwarfs* shows metamorphosis.

The Firm

Color, 1993
Running Time: 2 hours, 34 minutes
Rating: R
Distributor: *Paramount Pictures Corp.*

Mitch McDeere (Tom Cruise) graduates from Harvard Law School with honors. Many top law firms vigorously recruit him. Mitch chooses a small Memphis, Tennessee firm with a large starting salary, a new Mercedes, and a low-interest mortgage. He quickly learns that "The Firm" is entangled in a web of murder and corruption (Champoux 1999).

Scenes

Two sets of scenes show different stages of the socialization process. The first set shows the anticipatory stage before joining the company. The second set shows the entry/encounter stage after Mitch McDeere enters the firm.

1. Start: 0:04:52 — Stop: 0:17:23 — 13 minutes

This sequence starts at the beginning of the film and includes the credits. It ends after Mitch and Abby (Jean Trippelhorn) embrace following their discussion about accepting the firm's offer. Scenes have some R-rated language.

2. Start: 0:17:24 — Stop: 0:26:34 — 9 minutes

The second sequence starts at Abbey's school with her students giving her going away gifts. They end after Lamar Quinn (Terry Kinney) tells Mitch that the firm will pay his student loan. Lamar sits in a lawn chair, smoking and holding an unopened beer bottle, as the lawn sprinkler sprays him with water. He tells Mitch the firm will pay off his student loan. The film cuts to Abbey and Mitch driving away from Quinn's home. Scenes have some R-rated language.

What to Watch for and Ask Yourself

- What expectations does Mitch develop during the anticipatory stage of socialization?
- What expectations does Abby develop during their visit to Memphis? Should she share them more clearly with Mitch?
- Do you believe Mitch becomes fully socialized to "The Firm"?

Concepts or Examples

- ☐ Role episodes
- ☐ Pivotal role behaviors
- ☐ Stages of socialization (anticipatory, entry/encounter)
- ☐ Socialization processes (recruiting, recruitment interviews, mentoring, debasement experiences)

Analysis

_____

_____

_____

_____

_____

_____

Personal Reactions

_____

_____

_____

_____

_____

The Hudsucker Proxy (II)

Color, 1994
Running Time: 1 hour, 51 minutes
Rating: PG
Distributor: *Warner Home Video*

This is another look at Norville Barnes (Tim Robbins), the mailroom clerk who becomes President of Hudsucker Industries and invents the hula-hoop and the Frisbee. For a description of this film and another scene discussion, see page 94.

Scene (Start: 0:16:35 — Stop: 0:21:14 — 5 minutes)

This scene starts as Norville Barnes enters the mailroom. It ends after he is given the "blue letter" to deliver. The movie cuts to an opening elevator door

What to Watch for and Ask Yourself

- Which stage of socialization is Norville experiencing?
- What are the sources of Norville's socialization experiences?
- Which role behavior does he learn: pivotal, relevant, or peripheral?

Concepts or Examples

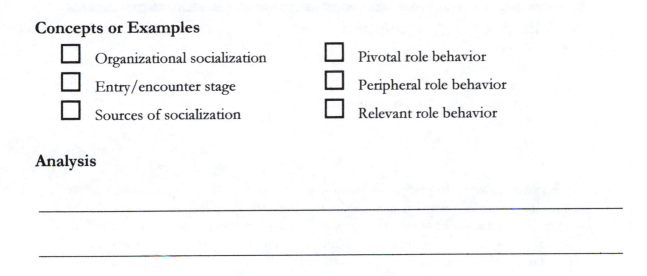

☐ Organizational socialization   ☐ Pivotal role behavior

☐ Entry/encounter stage   ☐ Peripheral role behavior

☐ Sources of socialization   ☐ Relevant role behavior

Analysis

_____

_____

_____

_____

_____

_____

Personal Reactions

_____

_____

_____

_____

_____

_____

An Officer and a Gentleman

Color, 1982
Running Time: 2 hours, 6 minutes
Rating: R
Distributor: *Paramount Pictures Corp.*

This film powerfully shows the training regimen of the Navy Officer Candidate School. Zack Mayo (Richard Gere) and the other candidates experience near torture at the hands of their drill instructor, Sergeant Emil Foley (Louis Gossett, Jr.). Zack, a loner, learns about discipline and dependence on others for success. The film is a dramatic and rough portrayal of the entry/encounter stage of socialization. It is rich in scenes showing debasement experiences—and features strong language and strong sexual references.

Scenes

There are two selected scenes. The first shows socialization experiences shortly after starting Officer Candidate School. The second shows the finished product at graduation after thirteen weeks of training.

1. Start: 0:21:58 — Stop: 0:28:54 — 7 minutes

This sequence starts with the shot of the candidates running through water and singing. It ends after Casey Seegar (Lisa Eilbacher) fails to scale the wall and Foley tells her to "Walk around! Walk around! Sugar britches." This scene cuts to a classroom scene.

2. Start: 1:55:33 — Stop: 1:59:25 — 4 minutes

The second sequence begins with the graduation ceremony, where the entire platoon assembles at attention in white uniforms. This scene follows the fight between Mayo and Foley. It ends after Mayo walks away after giving Foley a silver dollar. The film cuts to a shot of Mayo riding his motorcycle.

What to Watch for and Ask Yourself

- What is the purpose of debasement experiences during officer candidate training?
- What are some likely results?
- Are these results functional or dysfunctional for all involved?

Concepts or Examples

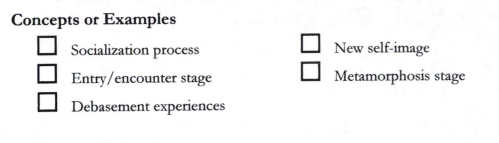

☐ Socialization process   ☐ New self-image

☐ Entry/encounter stage   ☐ Metamorphosis stage

☐ Debasement experiences

Analysis

_____

_____

_____

_____

_____

Personal Reactions

_____

_____

_____

_____

_____

Snow White and the Seven Dwarfs

Color, 1937
Running Time: 1 hour, 24 minutes
Rating: G
Distributor: *Walt Disney Home Video*

Walt Disney's first feature-length animated film adapts the famous Brothers Grimm fairy tale. The studio developed new animation techniques to get smooth character movement. To get further realism, Disney hired live actors as models (Connors and Craddock 2000, 837; Culhane 1986; Kanfer 1997).

The jealous Queen (Lucille La Verne), Snow White's stepmother, fears Snow White's beauty. She transforms herself into an old hag and convinces Snow White (Adriana Caselotti) to eat a poisoned apple. Snow White falls into the Sleeping Death that only a handsome Prince Charming's kiss can end. Her Seven Dwarf friends try to protect her in their forest house and stand watch over her sleep (Champoux in press).

Scene (Start: 0:52:42 — Stop: 0:55:50 — 3 minutes)

The scene starts with the Queen descending the stairs to her evil chamber. She has just learned that Snow White is alive and now wants to develop a way to kill her. It ends after the Queen's transformation into the old woman peddling apples. She leers at the audience, the screen goes black, and the film cuts to the Seven Dwarfs' house where everyone is singing.

What to Watch for and Ask Yourself

- Does the transformation of the Queen into the old hag symbolically show the result of the metamorphosis stage of socialization?
- Can metamorphosis in organizational socialization reach such extreme results in a real setting?
- What types of organizations feature such powerful socialization processes?

Concepts or Examples

☐ Metamorphosis

☐ Symbolism

☐ Result of metamorphosis stage of socialization

Analysis

_____

_____

_____

_____

_____

_____

Personal Reactions

_____

_____

_____

_____

_____

References

Champoux, J. E. 1999. Seeing and Valuing Diversity in Film. *Educational Media International* 36: 310-316. *Note:* Portions of this text have been used in this chapter with permission.

————. In press. Animated Films as a Teaching Resource. *Journal of Management Education. Note:* Portions of this text have been used in this chapter with permission.

Connors, M., and J. Craddock, eds. 2000. *VideoHound's Golden Movie Retriever.* Detroit: Visible Ink Press.

Culhane, S. 1986. *Talking Animals and Other People.* New York: St. Martin's Press.

Feldman, D. C. 1976. A Practical Program for Employee Socialization. *Organizational Dynamics* 5: 64–80.

————. 1981. The Multiple Socialization of Organization Members. *Academy of Management Review* 6: 309-318.

Fisher, C. 1986. Organizational Socialization: An Integrative Review. In *Research in Personnel and Human Resource Management*, vol. 4. Edited by K. M. Rowland and G. R. Ferris. Greenwich, CT: JAI Press, 101–145.

Kanfer, S. 1997. *Serious Business: The Art and Commerce of Animation in America from Betty Boop to Toy Story.* New York: Scribner.

Ott, J. S. 1989. *The Organizational Culture Perspective.* Pacific Grove, CA: Brooks/Cole.

Schein, E. H. 1968. Organizational Socialization and the Profession of Management. *Industrial Management Review* 9: 3.

Schein, E. H. 1992. *Organizational Culture and Leadership.* San Francisco: Jossey-Bass.

Trice, H. M., and J. M. Beyer. 1993. *The Cultures of Work Organizations.* Englewood Cliffs, NJ: Prentice-Hall.

Van Maanen, J., and E. H. Schein. 1977. Career Development. In *Improving Life at Work: Behavioral Science Approaches to Organizational Change.* Edited by J. R. Hackman and J. L. Suttle. Santa Monica: CA: Goodyear Publishing Company.

————. 1979. Toward a Theory of Organizational Socialization. In *Research in Organizational Behavior*, vol. 1. Edited by B. M. Staw and L. L. Cummings. Greenwich, CT: JAI Press, 209–264.

Motivation: Need Theories

Need theories of motivation propose psychological needs as a hypothetical concept to explain people's behavior. Needs are invisible characteristics of people that help shape their responses to different stimuli or objects in a person's environment. People can vary greatly in the pattern of needs that help guide their behavior (Evans 1986; Pinder 1998; Weimer 1992).

Some common needs are the need for affiliation and the need for achievement. The first need helps guide the social behavior of a person. A person with strong affiliation needs will likely interact with more people than would a person with a weak affiliation need. The need for achievement has strong ties to a person's successful work performance. Low achievers typically do not strive for as high a level of performance as high achievers.

Some theories propose need hierarchies, with some needs more important to a person's motivation than other needs. People move up and down their need hierarchy as they satisfy some needs (move upward) or become dissatisfied with others (move downward) (Alderfer 1972; Maslow 1943; Maslow, Stephens, and Heil 1998).

The following films, including some animated films, offer scenes showing various aspects of the need theories of motivation:

- Broadcast News
- The Odd Couple
- Toy Story
- The Many Adventures of Winnie the Pooh

Broadcast News shows two different people with different need structures. Felix Unger and Oscar Madison in *The Odd Couple* have vastly different need structures, making them a true odd couple. *Toy Story* offers a symbolic example of esteem needs, especially Buzz Lightyear's loss of self-esteem. *The Many Adventures of Winnie the Pooh* has a funny scene with Tigger about the need that motivates him.

Broadcast News (II)

Color, 1987
Running Time: 2 hours, 12 minutes
Rating: R
Distributor: *20th Century Fox Home Entertainment*

Camera-shy Aaron Altman (Albert Brooks) is a veteran reporter who reacts jealously to the handsome, hollow news anchor Tom Grunich (William Hurt)—both for career reasons and love interest Jane Craig (Holly Hunter), an over-achieving news producer. This smart comedy was nominated for seven Academy Awards. For other scenes and discussions of this film, see pages 134 and 264.

Scene (Start: 0:28:57 — Stop: 00:34:30 — 6 minutes)

This scene starts with Aaron Altman speaking Spanish to a Nicaraguan guerrilla. It ends after he runs down the stairs saying, "A year and half ago I made some stupid remark about his hairline. He's never gonna forget it." The film cuts to Tom Grunich talking on the telephone in his hotel room.

What to Watch for and Ask Yourself

- What needs motivate Jane?
- What is Aaron's need structure?
- Where is each of them in the hierarchy of needs?

Concepts or Examples

☐ Needs ☐ Growth needs

☐ Motivation ☐ Need for achievement

☐ Need for self-actualization ☐ Need hierarchy

Analysis

_____

_____

_____

_____

_____

_____

Personal Reactions

_____

_____

_____

_____

_____

_____

The Odd Couple (I)

Color, 1968
Running Time: 1 hour, 46 minutes
Rating: G
Distributor: *Paramount Pictures Corp.*

Neil Simon wrote the Broadway play from which this film is adapted. Two divorced men come to live together. Felix (Jack Lemmon) is fussy and neat, while his friend Oscar (Walter Matthau) is sloppy. Their mismatched living arrangement makes for many funny moments. For additional scenes and information about this film, see page 246.

Scene (Start: 0:34:38 — Stop: 0:40:55 — 6 minutes)

This scene, which follows the scene of Felix hyperventilating in Oscar's apartment, begins with Felix and Oscar walking down a street. Oscar is eating an ice-cream cone. It ends as Oscar and Felix leave a park bench and walk up some stairs. Oscar says to Felix, "You'll go on street corners and cry. They'll throw nickels at you. You'll work, Felix, you'll work."

What to Watch for and Ask Yourself

- What needs best fit Felix Ungar's behavior in this scene?
- What needs best fit Oscar Madison's behavior in this scene?
- Is the need pattern the same for the two people?

Concepts or Examples

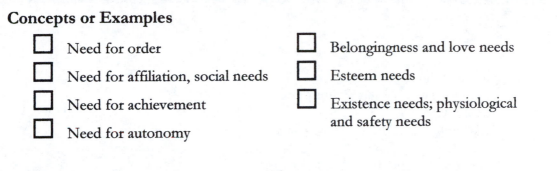

☐ Need for order

☐ Need for affiliation, social needs

☐ Need for achievement

☐ Need for autonomy

☐ Belongingness and love needs

☐ Esteem needs

☐ Existence needs; physiological and safety needs

Analysis

_____

_____

_____

_____

_____

Personal Reactions

_____

_____

_____

_____

_____

Toy Story

Color, 1995
Running Time: 1 hour, 21 minutes
Rating: G
Distributor: *Walt Disney Home Video*

This captivating and emotionally deep story tells what we have always imagined. Toys have a life and social organization of their own when humans are not present.

Andy's (John Morris) favorite toy is Sheriff Woody (Tom Hanks). He receives a new toy as a birthday gift, Buzz Lightyear, Space Ranger (Tim Allen). Buzz's presence disrupts the established social order, especially Woody's senior status among the toys. Concern about remaining as Andy's favorite induces conflict between Woody, Buzz, and the other toys. The tension increases because Buzz thinks he is a real space ranger, not a toy. Watch for the early scene of Mr. Potato Head (Don Rickles) calling the hockey puck a hockey puck! This was the first feature-length animated film created entirely with computer animation (Champoux in press).

Scene (Start: 1:06:54 — Stop: 1:10:50 — 4 minutes)

This scene starts with an outside shot of Sid's (Erik Von Detten) house during a thunderstorm. Woody needs Buzz's help to get out of a box. Buzz had seen a television commercial advertising him as a toy, his first sense of not being a real space ranger. The scene ends as Sid's alarm clock rings. It falls to the floor as Sid wakes up.

What to Watch for and Ask Yourself

- Do Woody and Buzz need each other to solve the problem of getting out of Sid's room?
- What is Buzz's level of self-esteem at this point?
- How does Woody motivate Buzz?

Concepts or Examples

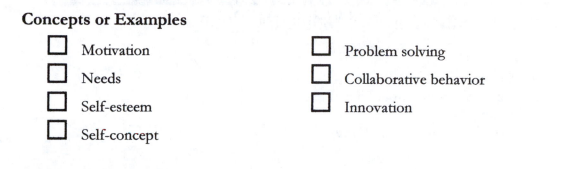

- ☐ Motivation
- ☐ Needs
- ☐ Self-esteem
- ☐ Self-concept

- ☐ Problem solving
- ☐ Collaborative behavior
- ☐ Innovation

Analysis

_____

_____

_____

_____

_____

Personal Reactions

_____

_____

_____

_____

_____

The Many Adventures of Winnie the Pooh

Color, 1977
Running Time: 1 hour 23 minutes
Rating: G
Distributor: *Walt Disney Home Video*

Disney's animated presentation of A. A. Milne's charming characters follows them through a series of adventures in the Hundred Acre Wood. Pooh, Piglet, Tigger, Rabbit, and the others offer engaging performances. The recommended scenes are a visual symbol of motivation and needs (Champoux in press).

Scenes (Start: 1:16:32 — Stop: 1:22:21 — 6 minutes)

This sequence begins with Pooh and Piglet seeing something (Tigger) in a tree. Pooh says, "Look…look, Piglet. There's something in that tree over there." The sequence ends after Tigger's bouncing and he says, "I'm the only one." Tigger roars. The film cuts to an image of a storybook with the page opened to "Chapter X, In Which."

What to Watch for and Ask Yourself

- What needs, in a figurative sense, is Tigger trying to satisfy?
- What needs motivate Rabbit?
- Observe the changes in Tigger's behavior after his needs are frustrated. Did Tigger change again after he satisfied his basic need?

Concepts or Examples

☐ Motivation   ☐ "Bouncing need"

☐ Safety need   ☐ Belongingness and love needs

Analysis

_____

_____

_____

_____

_____

_____

Personal Reactions

_____

_____

_____

_____

_____

References

Alderfer, C. P. 1972. *Existence, Relatedness, and Growth: Human Needs in Organizational Settings*. New York: Free Press.

Champoux, J. E. In press. Animated Films as a Teaching Resource. *Journal of Management Education*. *Note:* Portions of this text have been used in this chapter with permission.

Evans, M. G. 1986. Organizational Behavior: The Central Role of Motivation. *Yearly Review of Management of the Journal of Management* 12: 203–222.

Maslow, A. H. 1943. A Theory of Human Motivation. *Psychological Review* 50: 370–396.

Maslow, A. H., with D. C. Stephens and G. Heil. 1998. *Maslow on Management*. New York: John Wiley & Sons.

Pinder, C. C. 1998. *Work Motivation in Organizational Behavior*. Upper Saddle River, NJ: Prentice Hall.

Weimer, B. 1992. *Human Motivation: Metaphors, Theories, and Research*. Newbury Park, CA: Sage Publications.

CHAPTER 23

Motivation: Job Design

Organizations and managers create a context within which employees can experience intrinsic rewards. Although managers can use extrinsic rewards directly, they have only indirect control over intrinsic rewards. A manager cannot tell an employee to experience intrinsic rewards such as self-esteem or self-actualization. The manager can only create a set of job experiences that lets employees experience such rewards.

Job design and job redesign allow managers to create intrinsically motivating work. The primary method of designing jobs well into the 20th century, however, used task specialization. People did small tasks repeatedly. Although such jobs could be done more efficiently, there also were many human costs. Jobs that had small, repeated tasks created boredom and dissatisfaction among those doing the jobs (Sheppard and Herrick 1972; Walker and Guest 1952). By the early 1940s we began to see different efforts to redesign work to reduce the negative effects of high specialization (Griffin 1982; Hackman and Oldham 1980; Oldham 1996).

Job rotation involved the same worker moving among different jobs. **Job enlargement** involved adding duties and tasks to a job. **Job enrichment** also repackaged duties, but the repackaging involved adding duties and tasks that increased worker autonomy and responsibility (Herzberg 1968).

The following films show aspects of intrinsic rewards and job design:

- Blue Collar
- Joe Versus the Volcano
- Modern Times
- Clockwatchers

Blue Collar shows images of assembly line work in an automobile plant. *Joe Versus the Volcano* has scenes that emphasize the effect of a negative work context on people's responses to their job's intrinsic qualities. *Modern Times* offers a satirical look through Charlie Chaplin's eyes at 1930s manufacturing jobs. *Clockwatchers* offers a satirical look at work from the perspective of four temporary workers.

Blue Collar

Color, 1978
Running Time: 1 hour, 54 minutes
Rating: R
Distributor: *MCA Videocassette Inc.*

The comedian Richard Pryor stars in this serious and harsh look at a Detroit auto assembly plant in Paul Schrader's directorial debut. Poor labor–management relations and the unrelenting assembly line drive some workers into crime. The scenes of working on the line are a striking portrayal of assembly line work.

Scenes (Start: 0:01:17 — Stop: 0:06:51 — 6 minutes)

These scenes start with the opening credits and a wide shot of an automobile factory. They end after Jenkins (George Memmoli) walks away from his supervisor saying, "C'mon, that's all you ever do is say, 'Tell my union rep,' huh, 'Tell my union rep.'" The film cuts to a union meeting. The scenes have some R-rated language.

What to Watch for and Ask Yourself

- How motivating and satisfying do you expect these jobs to be?
- Rate the work context satisfaction of these workers? Use a 1-to-7 scale, where 1 is low satisfaction and 7 is high satisfaction.
- Can assembly line technology directly affect job design? How?

Concepts or Examples

☐ Job design

☐ Technical process and job design

☐ Assembly line technology

☐ Intrinsic rewards

Analysis

_____

_____

_____

_____

_____

_____

Personal Reactions

_____

_____

_____

_____

_____

Joe Versus the Volcano

Color, 1990
Running Time: 1 hour, 42 minutes
Rating: PG
Distributor: *Warner Home Video*

"Once upon a time there was a guy named Joe who had a very lousy job…" This film's opening title screen gives a strong clue about a typical workday for Joe Banks (Tom Hanks). He has a bad job and perhaps an even worse work environment. Joe does not feel well and learns from his doctor that he has a rare disease that will kill him within a few months. He accepts a millionaire's offer of a South Sea Island vacation where he will live like a king. The bad part of the vacation comes when he learns he must jump into a local volcano as part of an island ritual.

Scenes (Start: 0:07:41 — Stop: 0:14:22 — 8 minutes)

These scenes start as Joe (Tom Hanks) comes around a corner in a hallway and punches his time card at the time clock. They end after Joe puts his hands to his face and you hear the voice-over, "Mr. Banks. Mr. Banks."

What to Watch for and Ask Yourself

- What features of Joe's work context could affect his reaction to his job?
- Are those features positive or negative in their effects?
- How would you rate Joe's satisfaction with his physical work environment, coworkers, and supervisor? Use a 1-to-7 scale, where 1 is low satisfaction and 7 is high satisfaction.

Concepts or Examples

☐ Work environment

☐ Job context

☐ Supervisory behavior

☐ Coworkers

☐ Effects on reactions to job characteristics

☐ Work context satisfaction

Analysis

_____

_____

_____

_____

_____

Personal Reactions

_____

_____

_____

_____

_____

Modern Times

Black and White, 1936
Running Time: 1 hour, 27 minutes
Rating: G
Distributor: CBS Fox *Video*

Charlie Chaplin wrote and directed this film, the last film he made with his Little Tramp character and his first with sound. It is an engaging satirical portrayal of factory work of the period. Chaplin works in a factory tightening bolts on some nondescript parts that endlessly flow by him. He cracks under the stress of this work and runs crazily through the factory. The entire film features Chaplin trying to rebuild his life around the lovely Paulette Goddard. They eventually give up in the city and search for a better life elsewhere.

Scene (Start: 0:05:09 — Stop: 0:09:30 — 5 minutes)

This scene starts after the opening credits with a screen showing the text, "Modern Times. A story of industry, of individual enterprise—humanity crusading in the pursuit of happiness." It ends where Chaplin takes his break and lights a cigarette in the bathroom.

What to Watch for and Ask Yourself

- Predict a Motivating Potential Score (MPS) for these jobs. Using a seven-point scale, the lowest MPS is 1 and the highest is 343.
- How do you rate the work context? Use a 1-to-7 scale, where 1 is poor and 7 is great.
- Does the Job Characteristics Theory of Work Motivation predict the behavior shown in the scene?

Concepts or Examples

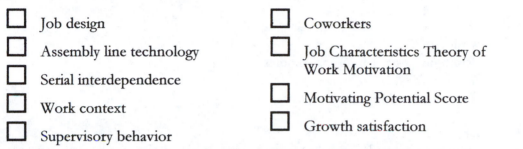

- ☐ Job design
- ☐ Assembly line technology
- ☐ Serial interdependence
- ☐ Work context
- ☐ Supervisory behavior

- ☐ Coworkers
- ☐ Job Characteristics Theory of Work Motivation
- ☐ Motivating Potential Score
- ☐ Growth satisfaction

Analysis

_____

_____

_____

_____

_____

Personal Reactions

_____

_____

_____

_____

_____

Clockwatchers

Color, 1997
Running Time: 1 hour, 32 minutes
Rating: PG-13
Distributor: *BMG Independents*

Jill Sprecher's directed this "slackerette" comedy about the underemployed and motivationally challenged, which stars Parker Posey and Lisa Kudrow, actors who have made a reputation in other amusing independent films about Generation X.

Scenes

There are two scenes in this film that satirize the work life of temporary workers and explore other aspects of working. Each has strong symbolic meaning about work.

1. Start: 0:09:58 — Stop: 0:15:28 — 5 minutes

These scenes start with Iris (Toni Collette) waiting for the reception clerk to notice her. The clock slowly ticks to 9 a.m., at which point the clerk asks if he can help. It ends with Iris repeatedly stamping "Urgent" on envelopes. The movie cuts to Iris boarding a bus.

2. Start: 0:24:34 — Stop: 0:25:17 — 2 minutes

This scene starts with Iris sitting at her desk watching the clock. It ends after the clock strikes 5 p.m. and the four temporary workers leave the building.

What to Watch for and Ask Yourself

- What are your feelings about the jobs of the four temporary workers?
- Could such jobs exist in the real world?
- What levels of intrinsic motivation and job satisfaction do you predict for each worker?

Concepts or Examples

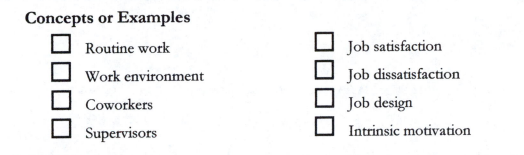

- ☐ Routine work
- ☐ Work environment
- ☐ Coworkers
- ☐ Supervisors
- ☐ Job satisfaction
- ☐ Job dissatisfaction
- ☐ Job design
- ☐ Intrinsic motivation

Analysis

_____

_____

_____

_____

_____

_____

Personal Reactions

_____

_____

_____

_____

_____

References

Griffin, R. W. 1982. *Task Design: An Integrative Approach.* Glenview, IL: Scott, Foresman.

Hackman, J. R., and G. Oldham. 1980. *Work Redeisgn.* Reading, MA: Addison-Wesley.

Herzberg, F. 1968. One More Time: How Do You Motivate Employees? *Harvard Business Review* (January–February): 53-62.

Oldham, G. R. 1996. Job Design. Ch. 2 in *International Review of Industrial and Organizational Psychology.* Edited by C. L. Cooper and I. T. Robertson. Chichester, England: John Wiley & Sons, Ltd.

Sheppard, H. L., and N. Q. Herrick. 1972. *Where Have All the Robots Gone?* New York: Free Press.

Walker, C. R., and R. Guest. 1952. *The Man on the Assembly Line* Cambridge, MA: Harvard University Press.

Groups and Teams

Groups can powerfully affect people's behavior. Knowledge of how and why groups form, and an understanding of their dynamics, can help you function better within a group or manage group activities (Levine and Moreland 1990).

A group is a collection of people trying to do a task or reach a goal. The people regularly interact with each other and depend on each other to do their tasks. The degree of mutual dependence is a function of the design of jobs the people are doing and the design of the organization (Wexley and Yukl 1977, 123).

Formal groups are either functional groups within an organization or task groups (Cartwright and Zander 1960, 36–38; Hare 1992). Functional groups are clusters of people formed by the design of the organization into departments and work units. Such groups are often permanent, but may change if the organization redesigns its structure.

Interaction patterns within organizations can affect the formation of informal groups within and across formal groups. Informal groups may form along interest lines, such as the task specialization of individuals, hobbies, or other concerns. Such groups form a "shadow organization" exerting powerful forces, both good and bad, on the formal organization (Allen and Pilnick, 1973).

The scenes described in this chapter show groups and intergroup processes in action. Scenes included here come from:

- Lifeboat
- The Dirty Dozen
- Hoosiers
- Le Mans

Lifeboat has some gripping opening scenes that show aspects of group formation. *The Dirty Dozen* shows a cohesive group in action. *Hoosiers* offers contrasting scenes about groups and group dynamics. The pit stop sequences in *Le Mans* show the performance of a group doing interdependent tasks.

Lifeboat

Black and White, 1944
Running Time: 1 hour, 37 minutes
Rating: NR
Distributor: *Key Video*

Alfred Hitchcock shot this remarkable film entirely in a single lifeboat.[*] The film chronicles the survival efforts of a shipwrecked group of people with diverse personalities. Set in World War II, the film takes many turns as it shows their interpersonal reactions in limited space. Differences among the people contribute to many dynamics and lead to some unexpected Hitchcockian results. Remade with a futuristic theme as *Lifepod* (1993).

Scenes (Start: 0:04:44 — Stop: 0:15:58 — 11 minutes)

These scenes start after the opening credits with a shot of the sinking freighter's smoke stack. The camera pans across floating debris and settles on a single person sitting in a lifeboat. The scenes end after the group pulls the German aboard and he says, "Danke schön." The screen goes black.

What to Watch for and Ask Yourself

- Which stage of group development do these scenes show?
- Did people in the scenes show behaviors typical for the stage you identified? Give some examples.
- What do you predict will be the result of this group? Cohesive? Not cohesive?

---

[*] Originally suggested to me by Glenn E. Kreiner, Doctoral Student, Department of Management, Arizona State University. — J.E.C.

Concepts or Examples

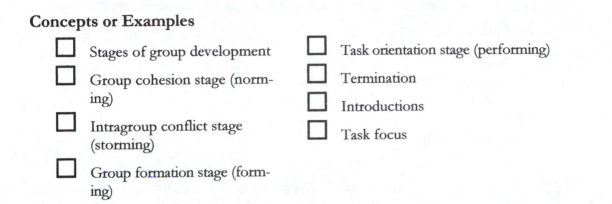

☐ Stages of group development

☐ Group cohesion stage (norming)

☐ Intragroup conflict stage (storming)

☐ Group formation stage (forming)

☐ Task orientation stage (performing)

☐ Termination

☐ Introductions

☐ Task focus

Analysis

_____

_____

_____

_____

_____

_____

Personal Reactions

_____

_____

_____

_____

_____

_____

The Dirty Dozen (II)

Color, 1967
2 hours, 30 minutes
Rating: NR
Distributor: *MGM/UA Home Video*

This adventure, set during World War II just before the Normandy Invasion, tells the tale of how twelve Army criminals redeem themselves in a daring raid behind enemy lines. See page 98 for another description of this film and an additional scene discussion.

Scenes (Start: 1:14:53 — Stop: 1:21:35 — 7 minutes)

A jeep pulls up to the gate of the Dirty Dozen's compound and the MP says, "This is a restricted area, Sir." The sequence ends after Colonel Breed (Robert Ryan) and his troops leave the compound. Two of Colonel Breed's men had earlier beaten Wadislaw (Charles Bronson). The film cuts to a shot of General Warden (Ernest Borgnine) and a heated discussion about the behavior of Major Reisman's men.

What to Watch for and Ask Yourself

- Is the Dirty Dozen a cohesive group? Why or why not?
- What function does this group serve for its members?
- Is their behavior dysfunctional for their organization, the U.S. Army?

Concepts or Examples

- [ ] Groups
- [ ] Cohesiveness
- [ ] Norms
- [ ] Conformity to group norms
- [ ] Functions of groups
- [ ] Superordinate goal

Analysis

_____

_____

_____

_____

_____

Personal Reactions

_____

_____

_____

_____

_____

Hoosiers

Color, 1987
Running Time: 1 hour, 55 minutes
Rating: PG
Distributor: *Avid Home Entertainment*

New high school basketball coach Norman Dale (Gene Hackman) transforms a losing team into a tournament-winning team. He is a former college coach forced out of coaching eleven years earlier. The setting is 1950s basketball-loving Indiana. This film chronicles the transformation of a small-town team unaccustomed to change into one with a succession of wins.

Scenes

There are two sets of scenes. The first set shows the team's behavior before the new coach arrives. The second set shows the result of the coach's efforts.

1. Start: 0:09:20 — Stop: 0:19:25 — 10 minutes

These scenes start with Norman Dale, the new coach, meeting some townspeople in the barbershop. The scene's opening dialogue says, "The last time you coached was . . . twelve years ago?" They end after the practice session in the gym. The movie cuts to a street scene and then a cafe with Dale and principal Cletus Summer (Sheb Wooley) drinking coffee.

2. Start: 1:33:36 — Stop: 1:50:01 — 17 minutes

The second set of scenes begins at the state tournament. A door to Butler Field House rises. Coach Dale and the players enter. They end after the wide shot of cheering fans on the playing floor. The movie fades to a sunset scene.

What to Watch for and Ask Yourself

- What factors contributed to the lack of cohesiveness of the team before the new coach arrived?
- How did the coach transform the team to a cohesive, winning team?
- What were the norms of this cohesive group?

Concepts or Examples

☐ Group dynamics   ☐ Formation of a cohesive group

☐ Cohesiveness   ☐ High-performance team

☐ Norms

Analysis

_____

_____

_____

_____

_____

Personal Reactions

_____

_____

_____

_____

_____

Le Mans

Color, 1971
Running Time: 1 hour, 46 minutes
Rating: G
Distributor: *CBS Fox Video*

This Steve McQueen film features dramatic real footage of the legendary Le Mans 24-hour Grand Prix endurance race. Michael Delaney (Steve McQueen) drops out of the race after crashing his car. Team manager David Townsend (Ronald Leigh-Hunt) asks Michael if he feels well enough to reenter the race in its final eight minutes. Townsend wants the Gulf Porsche team to win and they do. The team's pit crew works in a high-pressure, interdependent environment to get the victory.

Scenes

There are two sets of scenes at different points. The first set shows a pit crew in action on a Gulf Porsche team car. The second set shows victory for the team.

1. Start: 0:49:53 — Stop: 0:53:04 — 3 minutes

These scenes start with a shot of a loudspeaker announcing two car accidents including Michael's Gulf Porsche car. Team manager Townsend says "Bring them in for rain tires." The scenes end with Townsend's assistant checking a stopwatch and Townsend watching the car leave the pit.

2. Start: 1:41:04 — Stop: 1:44:13 — 3 minutes

The second set of scenes shows the race's end. It starts with a shot of a checkered flag. They end after team manager David Townsend thanks Michael.

What to Watch for and Ask Yourself

- Does this type of work require a team approach or could a single person do it?
- Is this a cohesive group? If so, what are its likely norms of behavior?
- What helped the Gulf Porsche team succeed in getting their car out of the pit before the Ferrari team?

Concepts or Examples

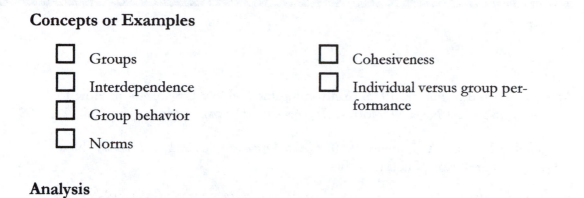

☐ Groups
☐ Interdependence
☐ Group behavior
☐ Norms

☐ Cohesiveness
☐ Individual versus group performance

Analysis

_____

_____

_____

_____

_____

_____

Personal Reactions

_____

_____

_____

_____

_____

_____

References

Allen, R. F., and S. Pilnick. 1973. Confronting the Shadow Organization: How to Detect and Defeat Negative Norms. *Organizational Dynamics* 1 (Spring): 6–10.

Cartwright, D., and A. Zander. 1960. *Group Dynamics: Research and Theory.* New York: Harper & Row, Publishers, Inc.

Hare, A. P. 1992. *Groups, Teams, and Social Interaction: Theories and Applications.* New York: Praeger.

Levine, J. M., and R. L. Moreland. 1990. Progress in Small Group Research. In *Annual Review of Psychology*, vol. 41. Edited by M. R. Rosensweig and L. W. Porter. Palo Alto, CA: Annual Reviews Inc., 585–634.

Wexley, K., and G. A. Yukl. 1977. *Organizational Behavior and Personnel Psychology.* Homewood, IL: Richard D. Irwin.

CHAPTER 25

Conflict and Conflict Management

Broadly defined, conflict behavior ranges from doubt or questioning to annihilation of an opponent (Robbins 1974, 23). A narrower definition says conflict in organizations is opposition, incompatible behaviors, or antagonistic interaction (Tjosvold 1991, 33). Conflict in organizations includes interactions in which one party opposes another party, or one party tries to prevent or block another party from reaching his or her goals. Critical elements of conflict are interdependence with another party and the perception of incompatible goals. The parties in conflict can be individuals or entire groups within the organization (Brown 1983; Rubin, Pruitt, and Kim 1994).

Conflict can happen in a series of episodes. As the conflict episodes ebb and flow, periods of cooperation may occur (Pondy 1967).

Conflict in organizations can serve useful functions when properly managed. Cooperation is not the only desirable state within an organization. Having cooperation without any conflict could result in a stagnant organization and complacent management (Robbins 1974, 28).

Four movies discussed in this chapter offer excellent scenes showing different aspects of conflict and conflict management:

- Fried Green Tomatoes
- Butch Cassidy and the Sundance Kid
- The Odd Couple
- 12 Angry Men

Fried Green Tomatoes has a short, effective scene that shows some important elements of a conflict episode. A scene from *Butch Cassidy and the Sundance Kid* shows all aspects of a conflict episode. *The Odd Couple* offers some humorous scenes that show how two different personalities chose to reduce their conflict. The scenes from *12 Angry Men* superbly show conflict episodes and the links between them.

Fried Green Tomatoes

Color, 1991
Running Time: 2 hours, 10 minutes
Rating: PG-13
Distributor: *MCA Universal Home Video*

Repressed Southern housewife Evelyn Couch (Kathy Bates) happens to meet the spry, elderly Ninnie Threadgoode (Jessica Tandy) at a nursing home. Ninnie's story of two women who lived fifty years earlier inspires Evelyn to take charge of her life. She develops into a more independent person determined to improve her boring marriage.

Scene (Start: 1:18:38 — Stop: 1:20:46 — 2 minutes)

This scene opens in the Winn-Dixie store parking lot. They follow the scenes in which Igie Threadgoode (Mary Stuart Masterson) and Ruth Jamison (Mary-Louise Parker) are talking about Frank's death. The scene fades from a shot of Ruth's face to the parking lot. Evelyn Couch is looking for a parking spot. The scene ends as the movie cuts to a shot of the nursing home.*

What to Watch for and Ask Yourself

- Did Evelyn expect to enter a conflict episode in the Winn-Dixie parking lot?
- What was the basis of the latent conflict in the episode?
- Describe the manifest conflict? What did Evelyn do to end the conflict episode?

---

*Recommended by Laura Dufek, my student at The Robert O. Anderson Graduate School of Management, The University of New Mexico. — J.E.C.

Concepts or Examples

☐ Manifest conflict   ☐ Perceived conflict

☐ Latent conflict   ☐ Conflict episode

☐ Felt conflict   ☐ Conflict aftermath

☐ Conflict reduction   ☐ Conflict Orientation

Analysis

_____

_____

_____

_____

_____

Personal Reactions

_____

_____

_____

_____

_____

Butch Cassidy and the Sundance Kid (III)

Color, 1969
Running Time: 1 hour, 12 minutes
Rating: PG
Distributor: *Fox Video*

The script of *Butch Cassidy and the Sundance Kid*, by William Goldman, is so sharp that you hang onto every line of dialogue. See pages 84 and 112 for descriptions of this film and discussions of other scenes.

Scenes (Start: 0:11:45 — Stop: 0:17:38 — 7 minutes)

This sequence starts with Butch Cassidy (Paul Newman) and the Sundance Kid (Robert Redford) riding through a river on their return to the gang's hideout in Hole-in-the-Wall, Wyoming. Butch says, "Boy you know every time I see Hole-in-the-Wall again, it's like seein' it . . . for the first time." The sequence ends after Butch says, "Harvey thought of that! Well I'll tell you something fellas, that's exactly what we're gonna do." The movie cuts to the sound of a steam locomotive.*

What to Watch for and Ask Yourself

- Does Butch Cassidy slowly perceive that a conflict episode is beginning? What is the evidence?
- What is the latent conflict in these scenes?
- What method of conflict reduction does he use? Will it likely end the episode with no conflict aftermath?

---

*Scenes recommended by Prof. Robert Eder of Portland State University. — J.E.C.

Concepts or Examples

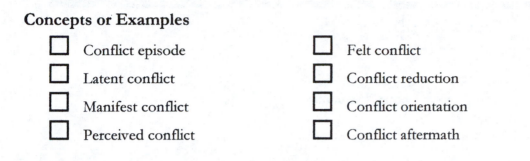

☐ Conflict episode ☐ Felt conflict

☐ Latent conflict ☐ Conflict reduction

☐ Manifest conflict ☐ Conflict orientation

☐ Perceived conflict ☐ Conflict aftermath

Analysis

_____

_____

_____

_____

_____

Personal Reactions

_____

_____

_____

_____

_____

The Odd Couple (II)

Color, 1968
Running Time: 1 hour, 46 minutes
Rating: G
Distributor: *Paramount Pictures Corp.*

The characters of Oscar, the lovable slob, and his friend Felix, the punctilious fanatic, have appeared in a successful television series and in a sequel that was not made until 30 years after the original. For an additional description and discussion of this film, see page 204.

Scenes (Start: 1:24:02 — Stop: 1:35:54 — 12 minutes)

The scenes start with the sound of Felix (Jack Lemmon) vacuuming. They end after they both reenter the apartment building from the roof with Oscar (Walter Mathau) saying, "Let what be on my head? Huh?"

What to Watch for and Ask Yourself

- What is the basis of the latent conflict?
- What behavior is the manifest conflict?
- What conflict reduction method did they use?

Concepts or Examples

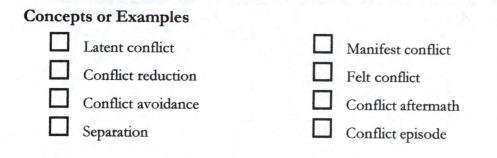

☐ Latent conflict   ☐ Manifest conflict

☐ Conflict reduction   ☐ Felt conflict

☐ Conflict avoidance   ☐ Conflict aftermath

☐ Separation   ☐ Conflict episode

Analysis

_____

_____

_____

_____

_____

Personal Reactions

_____

_____

_____

_____

_____

_____

12 Angry Men

Black and White, 1957
Running Time: 1 hour, 33 minutes
Rating: NR
Distributor: *MGM/UA Home Video*

This film—the directorial debut of Sidney Lumet—dramatically shows the struggle of twelve jurors trying to reach a verdict in a murder trial. The defendant is a young Hispanic man. Henry Fonda believes the defendant is innocent from the beginning of deliberations and presses for a not guilty verdict.

The characters—who are not named in the film—add to the dynamics of the conflict episodes portrayed. They include an impatient baseball fan with tickets to a game that night (Jack Warden); a logical, structured stockbroker (E. G. Marshall); a bigot (Ed Begley); and Fonda's chief opponent, a messenger service owner (Lee J. Cobb). The selected scenes show the final stages of decision.

Scenes (Start: 1:13:35 — Stop — 1:33:20 — 21 minutes)

These scenes start with a juror rising from his seat saying, "There is something I would like to say. I mean it's been bothering me a little ..." He is holding a switch blade knife. This scene tries to clarify the direction of the stabbing. The vote just before this scene was six to six, a possibly deadlocked jury in a murder trial. The scenes end after Lee J. Cobb's sobbing statement of "not guilty."

What to Watch for and Ask Yourself

- What are the start and stop points of each conflict episode?
- What is the content of each episode's conflict aftermath that becomes the latent conflict for the next episode?
- Which conflict reduction method finally ends the conflict among the jurors?

Concepts or Examples

- ☐ Conflict episodes
- ☐ Latent conflict
- ☐ Felt conflict
- ☐ Manifest conflict

- ☐ Conflict aftermath
- ☐ Links between conflict episodes
- ☐ Conflict reduction
- ☐ Conflict orientation

Analysis

_____

_____

_____

_____

_____

Personal Reactions

_____

_____

_____

_____

_____

References

Brown, L. D. 1983. *Managing Conflict at Organizational Interfaces*. Reading, MA: Addison-Wesley.

Pondy, L. R. 1967. Organizational Conflict: Concepts and Models. *Administrative Science Quarterly* 12: 296–320.

Robbins, S. P. 1974. *Managing Organizational Conflict*. Englewood Cliffs, NJ: Prentice Hall.

Rubin, J. Z., D. G. Pruitt, and S. H. Kim. 1994. *Social Conflict: Escalation, Stalemate, and Settlement*. New York: McGraw-Hill.

Tjosvold, D. 1991. *The Conflict-Positive Organization: Stimulate Diversity and Create Unity*. Reading, MA: Addison-Wesley Longman.

CHAPTER 26

Communication Processes

Organizational communication includes the purpose, flow, and direction of messages and the media used for them. Such communication happens within the complex, interdependent social systems of organizations. Think of communication as another view of behavior in organizations, which includes sending, receiving, and giving meaning to messages (Goldhaber 1993; Knapp and Hall 1997, Ch. 2; Porter and Roberts 1976).

Communication processes in organizations are continuous and constantly changing. They do not have a beginning or an end, nor do they follow a strict sequence. During communication, the sender creates messages from one or more symbols to which the sender attaches meaning. Messages can be oral, written, or nonverbal; they can also be intentional or unintentional.

Organizational communication happens over a pathway called a *network*. The network can be formal, as defined by formal organizational positions and relationships among those positions. It can also be informal as defined by informal patterns of social interaction. Communication over the network goes in any direction: downward, upward, or horizontal (Shannon and Weaver 1949).

Distortions, errors, and foreign material often affect the quality of the signal. Such noise is an addition to the signal not intended by the sender.

The following four films offer effective scenes showing different aspects of communication:

- Milk Money
- My Cousin Vinnie
- ¡Three Amigos!
- The Naughty Nineties ("Who's on First?")

Milk Money and *My Cousin Vinnie* show how different frames of reference affect communication accuracy. The "plethora" scene from *¡Three Amigos!* quickly notes how large words do not communicate well. Abbott and Costello's classic "Who's on First?" skit has no parallel for showing communication misunderstandings.

Milk Money

Color, 1994
Running Time: 1 hour, 50 minutes
Rating: PG-13
Distributor: *Paramount Pictures Corp.*

Three young boys with high sexual curiosity sell their possessions to get enough money to go to the city. They search for a woman who will show them her nude body. After several false starts and having their bicycles stolen, they meet V (Melanie Griffith), a prostitute. She returns them to their rural town using her pimp's car, which, unknown to her, has his hidden money. The car breaks down in front of young Frank Wheeler's (Michael Patrick Carter) house. His father, Tom Wheeler (Ed Harris) tries to repair her car.

Scenes (Start: 0:35:41 — Stop: 0:39:44 — 4 minutes)

These scenes start with Frank greeting Dad at the front door. He introduces V to his father as "Brad's new math tutor." They end after Tom Wheeler's futile efforts to start V's car. V says, "Poor man" as she kisses his cheek. V walks away and Wheeler looks bewildered while holding the jumper cables. The film cuts to V crossing the street.

What to Watch for and Ask Yourself

- What is the basis of the misperception shown in these scenes?
- What affect does that misperception have on the communication process?
- Was there any nonverbal communication that would have helped Dad better understand the situation?

Concepts or Examples

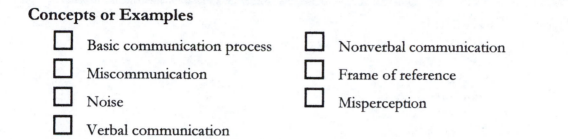

☐ Basic communication process   ☐ Nonverbal communication

☐ Miscommunication   ☐ Frame of reference

☐ Noise   ☐ Misperception

☐ Verbal communication

Analysis

_____

_____

_____

_____

_____

Personal Reactions

_____

_____

_____

_____

_____

_____

My Cousin Vinnie

Color, 1992
Running Time: 2 hours
Rating: R
Distributor: *Fox Video*

Former Brooklyn automobile mechanic Vincent Gambini (Joe Pesci) gets his first case after passing his bar examination on the sixth try.* His cousin Bill Gambini (Ralph Macchio) retains him as his defense attorney in his trial for murdering a store clerk. Vincent Gambini has no court experience. His courtroom demeanor reflects his Brooklyn streetwise behavior, putting him into almost constant conflict with the conservative judge (Fred Gwynn).

Scenes (Start: 0:08:44 — Stop: 0:15:17 — 6 minutes)

These scenes start as Bill Gambini and Stan Rothenstein (Mitchell Whitfield) drive up to the Sac-O-Suds grocery store. They end after the overhead shot of them sitting on a bench in handcuffs. The scenes have some R-rated language.

What to Watch for and Ask Yourself

- What is the basis of the miscommunication shown in these scenes?
- Are Sheriff Farley (Bruce McGill), Bill, and Stan using the same frame of reference?
- Do these scenes show the cost of miscommunication?

---

*Brendan Young, my student at The Robert O. Anderson School of Management, The University of New Mexico, recommended these scenes. — J.E.C.

Concepts or Examples

☐ Miscommunication   ☐ Misperception

☐ Basic communication process   ☐ Frame of reference

☐ Noise

Analysis

_____

_____

_____

_____

_____

Personal Reactions

_____

_____

_____

_____

_____

¡Three Amigos!

Color, 1986
Running Time: 1 hour, 45 minutes
Rating: PG
Distributor: *HBO/Cannon Video*

A silent film comedy team, The Three Amigos, have a falling out with their studio. They receive a telegram from a desperate citizen of a small Mexican village asking their help in fighting a gang of bandits. The Three Amigos interpret the message as an invitation to perform for 100,000 pesos. A comedy of errors unfolds when they discover there is no performance and the bandits use real bullets, not blanks.

Scene (Start: 1:05:01 — Stop: 1:06:10 — 1 minute)

This scene starts as El Guapo (Alfonso Arau) rides into the village and says to Jeffe (Tony Plana), "Jeffe! The gentlemen arrived yet?" It ends with El Guapo grinning at Jeffe after their short exchange.

What to Watch for and Ask Yourself

- Does Jeffe quickly understand El Guapo's meaning of *plethora*? Why?
- Is this effective or ineffective communication? Why?
- What could El Guapo have done to improve his communication effectiveness?

Concepts or Examples

☐ Noise

☐ Miscommunication

☐ Effective communication

☐ Ineffective communication

☐ Functional communication

☐ Dysfunctional communication

☐ Improving communication effectiveness

Analysis

_____

_____

_____

_____

_____

Personal Reactions

_____

_____

_____

_____

_____

The Naughty Nineties ("Who's on First?")

Black and White, 1945
Running Time: 1 hour, 16 minutes
Rating: NR
Distributor: *MCA Universal Home Video*

Typical Abbott and Costello slapstick humor and verbal banter highlight this story of a Mississippi River paddle wheeler besieged by crooks. A highlight of this otherwise ordinary comedy is the first on-screen presentation of the duo's classic *Who's on First?* skit.* You can test your listening skills by trying to identify the names of each player and the player's position.

Scene (Start: 0:41:01 — Stop: 0:47:14 — 6 minutes)

The "Who's on First" scene starts as Dexter Broader (Bud Abbott) comes on stage with a baseball bat singing, *Take Me Out to the Ball Game*. Sebastian (Lou Costello) comes on stage selling peanuts. They end after Sebastian throws down the bat and leers at Dexter. The movie cuts to the *River Queen's* gambling hall.

What to Watch for and Ask Yourself

- Is this an example of functional or dysfunctional communication?
- Does either person listen to what the other says?
- Would active listening have helped their communication?

---

*An alternate source for this skit (in a slightly different form) is the collection, *Hey Abbott!* (United American Video, 1991). It is the last segment in the collection (1:02:59–1:09:55; 7). Milton Berle introduces this skit as the best comedy routine ever. It ends at a frozen shot of Abbott and Costello after Lou says, "And I don't give a darn!" Abbott replies, "That's our shortstop."

Concepts or Examples

☐ Functional communication ☐ Active listening

☐ Dysfunctional communication ☐ Noise

☐ Listening

Analysis

_____

_____

_____

_____

_____

Personal Reactions

_____

_____

_____

_____

References

Goldhaber, G. M. 1993. *Organizational Communication*. Madison, WI: Brown & Benchmark.

Knapp, M. L., and J. A. Hall. 1997. *Nonverbal Communication in Human Interaction*. Fort Worth, TX: Harcourt Brace College Publishers.

Porter, L. W., and K. H. Roberts. 1976. Communication in Organizations. In *Handbook of Industrial and Organizational Psychology*, ed. M. D. Dunnette. Chicago: Rand McNally, Inc., 1567.

Shannon, C. E., and W. Weaver. 1949. *The Mathematical Theory of Communication*. Urbana, IL: University of Illinois Press.

Stress in Organizations

S tress is an unavoidable feature of life, a worldwide phenomenon that appears in many cultures. A person experiences stress when the environment presents a constraint, an opportunity, or an excessive physical or psychological demand (Beehr 1991; Glaser and Kiecolt-Glaser 1994; Matteson and Ivancevich 1979; Quick and Quick 1984; Seyle 1983).

The words **stressor** or **stressors** refer to objects or events in a person's physical and social environment that can induce a stress response. Stressors can be present in any environment through which a person passes. Those environments include the work environment, the nonwork environment, and the surrounding social, economic, and cultural environment.

The presence of a stressor does not mean all people will react with a stress response. A person's perceptual process affects whether the presence of a stressor leads to a stress response One person may perceive a stressor as a challenge to overcome, another person perceives the same stressor as a threat.

Stress is not always bad. Some stress can energize and motivate a person to behave in desired ways. It can move a person toward valued results offered by the opportunity.

The following films offer humorous or dramatic portrayals of stress, stressors, and stress responses.

- Head Office
- Broadcast News
- The Paper
- Falling Down

Head Office shows stress and stress response in a hysterically comical way. *Broadcast News* has dramatic scenes that show distress—and eustress—responses. *The Paper* shows the interaction of work and nonwork roles in inducing a stress response. The traffic jam scene in *Falling Down* shows the effects of multiple stressors.

Head Office

Color, 1986
Running Time: 1 hour, 30 minutes
Rating PG-13
Distributor: *Thorn EMI/HBO Video*

This film presents a comic-satirical view of power and political behavior at the highest levels of an organization. Confusion surrounds the unexpectedly fast promotions of Jack Issel (Judge Reinhold). This lighthearted film offers many scenes of power, political behavior in organizations, and illustrations of ethics.

Scenes (Start: 0:08:16 — Stop: 0:12:42 — 4 minutes)

These scenes begin with Jack Issel getting out of bed. He picks up a Brooks Brothers box and prepares for his first day of work at INC. They end after Jane (Jane Seymour) reneges on the date with Frank Stedman (Danny DeVito) for that evening.

What to Watch for and Ask Yourself

- What are the stressors affecting Stedman? Can he remove them from his environment?
- Is Stedman experiencing the stress response? What evidence of the stress response appears in these scenes?
- Do these scenes show distress or eustress?

Concepts or Examples

☐ Stress

☐ Stressors

☐ Stress response

☐ Distress

☐ "Fight or flight"

☐ Eustress

Analysis

_____

_____

_____

_____

_____

_____

Personal Reactions

_____

_____

_____

_____

_____

Broadcast News (III)

Color, 1987
Running Time: 2 hours 12 minutes
Rating: R
Distributor: *20th Century Fox Home Entertainment*

This comedy features the love triangle between a neurotic television producer (Holly Hunter), news anchor hunk (William Hurt), and ace reporter (Albert Brooks). For additional descriptions and scenes from this film, see pages 134 and 202.

Scenes (Start: 0:22:38 — Stop: 0:26:57 — 4 minutes)

These scenes start in the editing-room. The sound-over for the lead-in is the squeal of a tape rewinding. They end after Aaron Altman (Albert Brooks) reviews the end of the tape with Bobby (Christian Clemonson), the tape editor, and says, "He did smile." The film cuts to the newsroom with Jane (Holly Hunter) and Tom (William Hurt) talking. These scenes nicely contrast with the distress in the *Head Office* scene.

What to Watch for and Ask Yourself

- What does this scene suggest about the role of the stress response in a person's behavior?
- Is this distress or eustress?
- Did success with the project help them recover from the stress response?

Concepts or Examples

☐ Stress

☐ Distress

☐ Stressors

☐ Effects of stress

☐ Eustress

☐ Stress response

Analysis

_____

_____

_____

_____

_____

Personal Reactions

_____

_____

_____

_____

_____

The Paper

Color, 1994
Running Time: 1 hour, 52 minutes
Rating: R
Distributor: *MCA Universal Home Video*

This engaging film shows the ethical dilemmas and stress of producing a daily newspaper, *The New York Sun*. Editor Henry Hackett (Michael Keaton) races against the clock to produce a story that describes a major police scandal that could send two young Black men to jail. He is in constant conflict with his managing editor Alicia Clark (Glenn Close), whose ambitions focus her more on budget control than running true stories. Hackett also has constant pressure from his wife Marty (Marisa Tomei), who is pregnant with their first child. She wants him to take a less demanding job and continually pushes for that while Hackett tries to get the story he wants (Champoux 1999).

Scene (Start: 0:38:11 — Stop: 0:42:25 — 4 minutes)

This scene begins with Henry Hackett entering his office and finding Dan McDougall (Randy Quaid) lying on his sofa. It ends after McDougall says to Henry and Marty, "You two take your time. I'm on the Sedona thing." He leaves the office and closes the door. Marty says, "God, I miss this place." The film cuts to a close-up shot of a box of donuts.

What to Watch for and Ask Yourself

- What are the sources of stressors affecting Henry Hackett?
- How could Henry Hackett manage the stress in his life?
- Do stressors from different sources affect each other or are they insulated?

Concepts or Examples

☐ Stress　　　　　　　　☐ Distress

☐ Stressors　　　　　　　☐ Eustress

☐ Sources of stressors　　☐ Stress response

Analysis

_____

_____

_____

_____

_____

Personal Reactions

_____

_____

_____

_____

_____

Falling Down

Color, 1993
Running Time: 1 hour, 53 minutes
Rating: R
Distributor: *Warner Home Video*

Bill Foster (Michael Douglas), a law-abiding white-collar worker, snaps while stuck in a Los Angeles freeway traffic jam. He leaves his car and goes on a violent rage, lashing at anyone who gets in his way. This film has many harrowing moments as Foster tries, by force, to return to the happy, normal life he never really had. His pursuer, Detective Pendergast (Robert Duvall), has one day before retirement but sets out to capture him.

Scene (Start: 0:03:19 — Stop: 0:07:40 — 5 minutes)

The scene starts after the title screen that reads, "A Joel Schumacher Film" and the camera slowly zooms back from a close-up of Foster's face. It ends after Foster runs off into the shrubs under a freeway. The movie cuts to a shot of Detective Pendergast sitting in his prowl car.

What to Watch for and Ask Yourself

- What are the stressors affecting Bill Foster?
- What were the psychological and physiological stress responses?
- Did Foster experience eustress of distress?

Concepts or Examples

☐ Stressors

☐ Stress response

☐ Physiological stress response

☐ Psychological stress response

☐ Eustress

☐ Distress

Analysis

_____

_____

_____

_____

_____

_____

Personal Reactions

_____

_____

_____

_____

_____

_____

References

Beehr, T. A. 1991. *Psychological Stress in the Workplace*. New York: Unwin Hyman Academic.

Champoux, J. E. 1999. Seeing and Valuing Diversity in Film. *Educational Media International* 36: 310–316. *Note:* Portions of this article have been adapted for this chapter. Used with permission.

Glaser, R., and J. Kiecolt-Glaser. 1994. *Handbook of Human Stress and Immunity*. San Diego: Academic Press.

Matteson, M. T., and J. M. Ivancevich. 1979. Organizational Stressors and Heart Disease: A Research Model. *Academy of Management Review* 4: 347–357.

Quick, J. C., and J. D. Quick. 1984. *Organizational Stress and Preventive Management*. New York: McGraw-Hill.

Selye, H. 1976. *The Stress of Life*. New York: McGraw-Hill.

CHAPTER 28

Organizational Change and Development

Organizational change involves movement from the present state of the organization to some future or target state (Beckhard and Harris 1987; Beckhard and Pritchard 1992; Beer and Walton 1987; Burke 1995; Goodstein and Burke 1991). The future state may be a new strategy for the organization, changes in the organization's culture, introduction of a new technology, and so on. Organizational change is either unplanned or planned. **Unplanned change** occurs when pressures for change overwhelm efforts to resist the change. Such change can be unexpected by management and result in uncontrolled change effects. **Planned change** involves systematic efforts by managers to move an organization, or a subsystem, to a new state. Planned change includes deliberately changing the organization's design, technology, tasks, people, information systems, and the like.

A consultant often serves as a *change agent* to help managers bring about planned organizational change. The consultant may be external to the organization or part of a staff function that specializes in helping managers carry out planned organizational change.

Scenes from the following films show different aspects of organizational change and development:

- The Coca-Cola Kid
- Local Hero
- Network
- The Efficiency Expert

The *Coca-Cola Kid*, an Australian film, shows a change agent who is not right for the target of change. *Local Hero*, a Scottish film, shows more complex aspects of organizational change and how a change agent was successful. *Network* shows some behavioral effects of a proposed organizational change. Four scenes from *The Efficiency Expert* form the basis of a predictive video case. View them in sequence to see the different stages of organizational change.

The Coca-Cola Kid

Color, 1985
Running Time: 1 hour, 38 minutes
Rating: R
Distributor: *Vestron Video*

This Australian film shows Becker's (Eric Roberts) frustrated efforts to bring an old soft drink bottling plant into modern times. Mr. T. George McDowell (Bill Kerr) resists Decker's efforts to convert him to manufacturing Coca-Cola. This comedy shows some wonderful footage of Australia and features a satirical look at Australian organizations and management practices.

Scene (Start: 0:37:15 — Stop: 0:42:03 — 5 minutes)

This scene starts with T. George McDowell's face rearing up on the screen as Becker arrives at the plant. Becker is dragging McDowell's hired killer behind the jeep. It follows Becker's encounter with the killer while traveling to the plant. The scene ends as Becker drives away following his discussion with T. George. The film cuts to a shot of a parrot.

What to Watch for and Ask Yourself

- Is Becker's approach to changing McDowell's factory likely to lead to major change?
- How should Becker approach McDowell?
- What do you predict is the result of Becker's efforts?

Concepts or Examples

☐ Organizational change

☐ Resistance to change

☐ Reasons for resistance

☐ Change agent

☐ Characteristics of change agent

Analysis

_____

_____

_____

_____

_____

_____

Personal Reactions

_____

_____

_____

_____

_____

Local Hero

Color, 1983
Running Time: 1 hour, 12 minutes
Rating: PG
Distributor: *Warner Home Video*

A large American oil company sends a young executive "Mac" MacIntyre (Peter Riegert) to a small Scottish coastal village to buy land for an oil refinery. The different—and seemingly odd—cultural traditions of the village people captivate and distract him from his primary goal. He does not move fast enough to please the company president, Felix Happer (Burt Lancaster), who arrives to close the deal. The lone hold out on selling land, old Ben Knox (Fulton MacKay), presents Mr. Happer with a true challenge. This unusual film has wonderful characters and beautiful views of the Scottish countryside.

Scenes (Start: 1:23:20 — Stop; 1:44:02 — 21 minutes)

These scenes, which follow MacIntyre's drunken conversation in a pub, start with a British fighter plane in flight and MacIntyre's voice-over saying, "You drive a car, Victor?" They end as Mr. Happer walks down the beach. The film cuts to MacIntyre paying his bill in the pub.

What to Watch for and Ask Yourself

- What is the basis of resistance to change shown in these scenes?
- What is Happer's approach to the resistance?
- Did any benefits accrue to all parties involved from Happer's final decision?

Concepts or Examples

☐ Resistance to change

☐ Reasons for resistance to change

☐ Manager's orientation to resistance to change

☐ Ways of reducing resistance to change

Analysis

_____

_____

_____

_____

_____

Personal Reactions

_____

_____

_____

_____

_____

Network (II)

Color, 1976,
Running Time: 1 hour, 56 minutes
Rating: R
Distributor: *MGM/UA Home Video*

Paddy Chayefsky's sardonic, Academy Award-winning screenplay examines how low a television network will go to boost ratings with its new live, violent "guerrilla television" programming. Another scene from this film is discussed on page 88.

Scenes (Start: 0:16:28 — Stop: 0:22:30 — 6 minutes)

These scenes follow a meeting in Diana Christensen's (Faye Dunaway) office and begin with the opening of the board of directors meeting, when Frank Hackett (Robert Duvall) says, "But, the business of management is management." They end after Edward Ruddy (William Prince), president of the Systems Group, sits in a chair rubbing his brow. These scenes have some R-rated language. The film cuts to a television set showing Howard Beale's (Peter Finch) news conference.

What to Watch for and Ask Yourself

- Does Hackett propose a major change in the design of the organization?
- Is there evidence of resistance to change?
- How could this process be managed to maximize the positive effects of any change?

Concepts or Examples

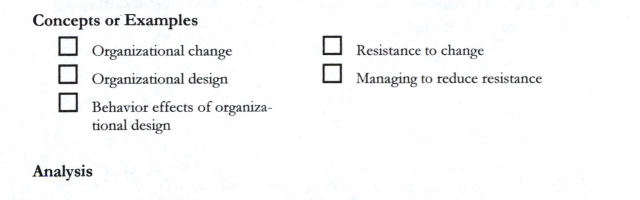

- ☐ Organizational change
- ☐ Organizational design
- ☐ Behavior effects of organizational design

- ☐ Resistance to change
- ☐ Managing to reduce resistance

Analysis

_____

_____

_____

_____

_____

_____

Personal Reactions

_____

_____

_____

_____

_____

The Efficiency Expert (I)

Color, 1992
Running Time: 1 hour, 37 minutes
Rating: PG
Distributor: *Paramount Pictures Corporation*

Balls Moccasin Company in Spottswood, Australia is losing money. A company interested in acquiring it sends a consultant to assess its condition and help it improve operations. The company's owner has sold assets over the years to cover its losses. The setting is 1960s Australia. Other scenes are discussed on the following pages.

Scenes (Start: 0:10:04 — Stop: 0:20:46 — 11 minutes)

These scenes start with cars entering the Balls Moccasin factory grounds. Consultant Errol Wallace (Sir Anthony Hopkins) enters the factory for his meeting with Mr. Ball (Alwyn Kurts). The scenes end after someone calls to Wallace. The movie cuts to two people wheeling a bicycle across a bridge.

What to Watch for and Ask Yourself

- What role does consultant Wallace expect to play in the planned change of Balls Moccasin Company?
- Which phase of the planned change process do these scenes show?
- How would you characterize Wallace's view of the management of this company?

Concepts or Examples

☐ Planned organizational change

☐ Change agent

☐ Diagnosing the present state of an organization

☐ Phases of planned change

Analysis

_____

_____

_____

_____

_____

Personal Reactions

_____

_____

_____

_____

_____

The Efficiency Expert (II)

For a description of this film, see page 278.

Scenes (Start: 0:33:34 — Stop: 0:37:50 — 5 minutes)

These scenes start with a shot of a left-handed person, Cary (Ben Mendelsohn), signing a letter. They end after Errol Wallace (Sir Anthony Hopkins) calls to Cary and asks him to go with him. The movie cuts to a shot of moccasins in a store window.

What to Watch for and Ask Yourself

- What stage of planned organizational change do these scenes show?
- What specific changes does Mr. Wallace recommend?
- How will the employees react to the proposed change?

Concepts or Examples

☐ Intervention   ☐ Change agent

☐ Planned organizational change   ☐ Reaction to change

Analysis

_____

_____

_____

_____

_____

_____

Personal Reactions

_____

_____

_____

_____

_____

The Efficiency Expert (III)

For a description of this film, see page 278.

Scene (Start: 0:53:07 — Stop: 0:57:13 — 4 minutes)

This scene opens on a Balls Moccasins sign on a car door. It ends after Cary (Ben Mendelsohn) fixes his bicycle tire. The movie cuts to a worker protest march.

What to Watch for and Ask Yourself

- What are the effects of Mr. Wallace's (Sir Anthony Hopkins) change efforts?
- What information could Wallace and Mr. Ball (Alwyn Kurts) learn from employee reactions to the changes?
- How could the consultant and management have reduced resistance to change?

Concepts or Examples

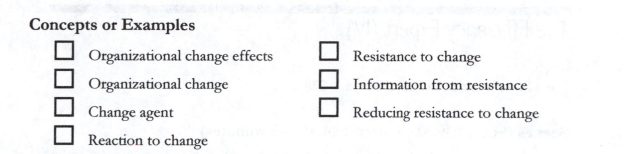

- ☐ Organizational change effects
- ☐ Organizational change
- ☐ Change agent
- ☐ Reaction to change

- ☐ Resistance to change
- ☐ Information from resistance
- ☐ Reducing resistance to change

Analysis

_____

_____

_____

_____

_____

Personal Reactions

_____

_____

_____

_____

_____

The Efficiency Expert (IV)

For a description of this film, see page 278.

Scenes (Start: 1:19:32 — Stop: 1:24:41 — 5 minutes)

These scenes begin with a shot of the cocktail party. The camera pans left to Errol Wallace (Sir Anthony Hopkins) standing with a drink in his hand. After Wallace and Mr. Ball (Alwyn Kurts) toast each other, the scene ends, and the film cuts to inside a movie theater. Cary (Ben Mendelsohn) enters and walks down the aisle. There is a brief intercut scene of the cocktail party with Cary talking to Cheryl Ball (Rebecca Rigg). (The word "pissed" is Australian (and British) slang for being drunk.)

What to Watch for and Ask Yourself

- What prompted the change in Mr. Wallace's approach to the company?
- Identify the major elements of Wallace's proposed changes. Can they have strong effects on Balls Moccasin employees' behavior?
- What are your predictions for the change? Success? Failure?

Concepts or Examples

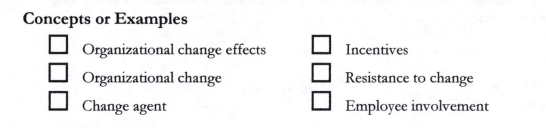

☐ Organizational change effects

☐ Organizational change

☐ Change agent

☐ Incentives

☐ Resistance to change

☐ Employee involvement

Analysis

_____

_____

_____

_____

_____

Personal Reactions

_____

_____

_____

_____

_____

References

Beckhard, R., and R. T. Harris. 1987. *Organizational Transitions: Managing Complex Change*. Reading, MA: Addison-Wesley Publishing Company, Inc.

Beckhard, R., and W. Pritchard. 1992. *Changing the Essence: The Art of Creating and Leading Fundamental Change in Organizations*. San Francisco: Jossey-Bass.

Beer, M., and A. E. Walton. 1987. Organizational Change and Development. In *Annual Review of Psychology*, vol. 38. Edited by M. R. Rosenzweig and L. W. Porter. Stanford, CA: Annual Reviews, 339–367.

Burke, W. W. 1995. Organization Change: What We Know, What We Need to Know. *Journal of Management Inquiry* 4: 158–171.

Goodstein, L. D., and W. W. Burke. 1991. Creating Successful Organizational Change. *Organizational Dynamics* 19 (Spring): 5–17.

Future Directions of Organizations and Management

The areas of future change include demographic and economic changes within the United States and major international changes. Changes in diplomacy and trade will increasingly emphasize a global view by managers and organizations in the future. Technological changes in information processing, materials, manufacturing, and transportation will also present exciting new challenges and opportunities. Managers of the future will forge new strategic plans to meet these challenges. Organizations of the future will take on a new look—flatter, more decentralized, and more flexible than they are now. Ethical issues and ethical decision making will loom large in the future, taking on global dimensions (Champoux 2000, Ch. 19).

This chapter discusses scenes from the following films:

- Rush Hour
- Gung Ho
- The Jetsons: First Episodes
- The General's Daughter

Rush Hour has a brief scene that emphases the role of diversity in the future. *Gung Ho* has an opening scene that nicely shows culture shock from international travel. The early episodes of the television program *The Jetsons* were surprisingly prescient about future technology. A late scene in *The General's Daughter* symbolizes the ethical dilemmas that will be a major feature of the future.

Rush Hour

Color, 1998
Running Time: 1 hour, 37 minutes
Rating: PG-13
Distributor: *New Line Home Video*

"South Central LA Meets Hong Kong" could have been an alternative title for this action packed comedy. Detective Carter (Chris Tucker) is assigned to keep Hong Kong detective Lee (Jackie Chan) away from an FBI investigation. The Chinese Consul's daughter has been kidnapped and the FBI does not want any help. Confusion and action range far as Lee presses to help his friend the Consul.

Scene (Start: 0:54:09 — Stop: 0:57:14 — 3 minutes)

This scene starts with Carter and Lee driving into Chinatown in Carter's black Corvette Stingray. They park by the Foo Chow restaurant. The scene ends as Carter and Lee do their LA stride down the street. The movie cuts to FBI agents talking about setting up bugs.

What to Watch for and Ask Yourself

- Are their examples of international diversity in these scenes?
- Do you see acceptance and valuing of diversity?
- Is there tension between Lee and Carter because of their differences? If yes, what are specific examples?

Concepts or Examples

☐ Diversity

☐ Valuing diversity

☐ Accepting diversity

☐ Sensitivity to differences

☐ Synergy from diversity

Analysis

_____

_____

_____

_____

_____

_____

Personal Reactions

_____

_____

_____

_____

_____

Gung Ho (II)

Color, 1986
Running Time: 1 hour, 51 minutes
Rating: PG-13
Distributor: *Paramount Home Video*

The title of this film alludes to a super-patriotic World War II-era film *Gung Ho!*, about American Marines taking on the Japanese Army—and winning. But the tables are turned in this film, when Assan Motors takes over a closed American automobile plant and tries to make its unionized workers adapt to Japanese management style.* See page 142 for a detailed description of this film and another scene discussion.

Scenes (Start: 0:00:57 — Stop: 0:11:56 — 11 minutes)

These scenes start after the Paramount logo, a dark screen, and sounds of screaming Japanese. The film cuts to Japanese managers in a shame training class. The scenes end as a dejected Stevenson (Michael Keaton) walks past a Japanese temple. The movie cuts to a plane arriving in Hadleyville.

What to Watch for and Ask Yourself

- Did Hunt Stevenson experience culture shock after arriving in Tokyo? If so, what elements of Japanese culture surprised him?
- Did he commit any cultural errors while trying to find the Assan Motors office?
- Did he commit any cultural errors while making his presentation to Assan Motors?

---

*First recommended by my student, Christopher J. van Lone, at the Robert O. Anderson School of Management, the University of New Mexico. — J.E.C.

Concepts or Examples

☐ Culture shock   ☐ Cultural insensitivity

☐ Cross-cultural errors   ☐ Offensive behavior

☐ Cultural sensitivity

Analysis

_____

_____

_____

_____

_____

_____

Personal Reactions

_____

_____

_____

_____

_____

The Jetsons: First Episodes

Color, 1989
Running Time: 1 hour, 30 minutes
Rating: NR
Distributor: *Hanna-Barbera Home Video*

This collection of four early Jetsons episodes features the arrival of Rosie the Robot and introduces the Jetson family members: George Jetson, his wife Jane, daughter Judy, and "his boy," Elroy. One episode shows Astro, the Jetson family dog, coming home with Elroy for the first time. These episodes originally aired in 1962. Many technology features in these episodes exist today or will exist soon.

Scenes (Start: 0:01:28 — Stop: 0:13:12 — 12 minutes)

These scenes start with the title screen that says, "Rosie the Robot." They end after George Jetson parks his saucer on the roof of his apartment building. He says, "I hate these compact saucers" as he walks to his apartment.

What to Watch for and Ask Yourself

- Which technologies shown in these scenes exist today?
- Which technologies will exist in the near future?
- Which technologies are still fantasies?

Concepts or Examples

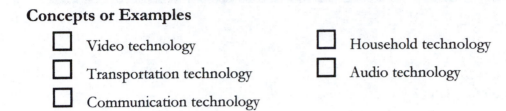

☐ Video technology   ☐ Household technology

☐ Transportation technology   ☐ Audio technology

☐ Communication technology

Analysis

_____

_____

_____

_____

_____

_____

Personal Reactions

_____

_____

_____

_____

_____

_____

The General's Daughter

Color, 1999
Running Time: 1 hour, 57 minutes
Rating: R
Distributor: *Paramount Pictures*

Paul Brenner (John Travolta), an Army investigator, is assigned to a murder and suspected rape case. Difficulties abound because the victim was the daughter of a famous, soon-to-retire General. Efforts to keep the case away from local police and the FBI create time pressures for Brenner and his associate Sunhill (Madeline Stowe). Based on Nelson DeMille's best-selling novel, the film takes many twisting turns to its unexpected ending.

Scene (Start: 1:39:23 — Stop: 1:46:10 — 7 minutes)

The scene begins as Brenner, in uniform, approaches Lieutenant General Campbell's (James Cromwell) quarters. They follow the review of the answering machine tape with the late Colonel Moore's lawyer (James Woods). The scene ends after Brenner removes a sheet of paper from his coat and says, "Names of the perpetrators my Associate Agent Sunhill found with a minimum of trouble. Apple pie, Sir."

What to Watch for and Ask Yourself

- Did General Campbell behave ethically or unethically in asking his daughter to forget her rape?
- Which ethical theory or view was the dominant one in Campbell's reasoning?
- Is their an alternative ethical theory or view that would have reached a different conclusion?

Concepts or Examples

☐ Ethical behavior

☐ Rights theory

☐ Utilitarianism

☐ Egoism

☐ Justice theory

☐ Unethical behavior

Analysis

_____

_____

_____

_____

_____

_____

Personal Reactions

_____

_____

_____

_____

_____

_____

References

Champoux, J. E. 2000. *Organizational Behavior: Essential Tenets for a New Millennium.* Cincinnati, OH: South-Western College Publishing.

Bibliography

Aho, C. M., and S. Ostry. 1990. Regional Trading Blocs: Pragmatic or Problematic Policy? In *The Global Economy: America's Role in the Decade Ahead,* ed. W. E. Brock and R. D. Hormats. New York: W. W. Norton, 147–173.

Alderfer, C. P. 1972. *Existence, Relatedness, and Growth: Human Needs in Organizational Settings.* New York: Free Press.

Allen, R. F., and S. Pilnick. 1973. Confronting the Shadow Organization: How to Detect and Defeat Negative Norms. *Organizational Dynamics* 1 (Spring): 6–10.

Allport, G. W. 1937. *Personality: A Psychological Interpretation.* New York: Henry Holt.

Alvesson, M., and P. O. Berg. 1992. *Corporate Culture and Organizational Symbolism.* New York: Hawthorne/Walter de Gruyter.

Ballesteros, S. 1994. Cognitive Approaches to Human Perception: Introduction. In *Cognitive Approaches to Human Perception.* Edited by S. Ballesteros. Hillsdale, NJ: Lawrence Erlbaum Associates.

Banner, D. K., and T. E. Gagne. 1995. *Designing Effective Organizations: Traditional and Transformational Views.* Thousand Oaks, CA: Sage Publications.

Barnard, C. I. 1938. *The Functions of the Executive.* Cambridge: Harvard University Press.

Barrick, M. R., and M. K. Mount. 1991. The Big Five Personality Dimensions and Job Performance: A Meta-Analysis. *Personnel Psychology* 44: 1–26.

Bass, B. M. 1990. *Bass & Stogdill's Handbook of Leadership: Theory, Research, & Managerial Applications.* New York: The Free Press.

Beckhard, R., and R. T. Harris. 1987. *Organizational Transitions: Managing Complex Change.* Reading, MA: Addison-Wesley Publishing Company, Inc.

Beckhard, R., and W. Pritchard. 1992. *Changing the Essence: The Art of Creating and Leading Fundamental Change in Organizations.* San Francisco: Jossey-Bass.

Beehr, T. A. 1991. *Psychological Stress in the Workplace.* New York: Unwin Hyman Academic.

Beer, M., and A. E. Walton. 1987. Organizational Change and Development. In *Annual Review of Psychology,* vol. 38. Edited by M. R. Rosenzweig and L. W. Porter. Stanford, CA: Annual Reviews, 339–367.

Bendazzi, G. 1994. *Cartoons: One Hundred Years of Cinema Animation.* Bloomington, IN: Indiana University Press.

Berlo, D. K. 1960. *The Process of Communication.* New York: Holt, Rinehart and Winston.

Blau, P. M., and W. R. Scott. 1962. *Formal Organizations.* San Francisco: Chandler Publishing Co.

Bond, M. A., and J. L. Pyle. 1998. The Ecology of Diversity in Organizational Settings: Lessons from a Case Study. *Human Relations* 51: 589–623.

Brandt, R. B. 1959. *Ethical Theory: The Problems of Normative and Critical Ethics.* Englewood Cliffs, NJ: Prentice Hall.

Brown, L. D. 1983. *Managing Conflict at Organizational Interfaces.* Reading, MA: Addison-Wesley.

Buchholz, R. A. 1989. *Fundamental Concepts and Problems in Business Ethics.* Englewood Cliffs, NJ: Prentice Hall.

Burke, W. W. 1995. Organization Change: What We Know, What We Need to Know. *Journal of Management Inquiry* 4: 158–171.

Butler, R. J. 1991. *Designing Organizations: A Decision-Making Perspective.* New York: Routledge.

Cairncross, F. 1998. *The Death of Distance.* Boston: Harvard Business School Press.

Cartwright, D., and A. Zander. 1960. *Group Dynamics: Research and Theory*. New York: Harper & Row, Publishers, Inc.

Champoux, J. E. 1999. Management Context of Not-for-Profit Organizations in the Next Millennium: Diversity, Quality, Technology, Global Environment, and Ethics. In *The Nonprofit Management Handbook*. 2d ed. 1999 supplement. Edited by T. D. Connors. New York: John Wiley & Sons, 7–9.

Champoux, J. E. 1999. Seeing and Valuing Diversity in Film. *Educational Media International* 36: 310–316.

Champoux, J. E. 2000. *Organizational Behavior: Essential Tenets for a New Millennium*. Cincinnati, OH: South-Western College Publishing.

Champoux, J. E. In press. Animated Film as a Teaching Resource. *Journal of Management Education*.

Connors, M., and J. Craddock, eds. 2000. *VideoHound's Golden Movie Retriever*. Detroit: Visible Ink Press.

Culhane, S. 1986. *Talking Animals and Other People*. New York: St. Martin's Press.

Davidoff, J. B. 1975. *Differences in Visual Perception: The Individual Eye*. London: Crosby Lockwood Stapes.

Davis, B., and J. Calmes. 1993. The House Passes Nafta—Trade Win: House Approves Nafta, Providing President With Crucial Victory. *Wall Street Journal* (November18): A1.

Davis, M. R., and D. A. Weckler. 1996. *A Practical Guide to Organization Design*. Menlo Park, CA: Crisp Publications.

Davis, P. E., ed. 1973. *Introduction to Moral Philosophy*. Columbus, Ohio: Charles E. Merrill Publishing Company.

Deal, T. E., and A. A. Kennedy. 1982. *Corporate Cultures: The Rites and Rituals of Corporate Life*. Reading, MA: Addison-Wesley.

Dember, W. N., and J. S. Warm. 1979. *Psychology of Perception*. New York: Holt, Rinehart and Winston.

Digman, J. M. 1990. Personality Structure: Emergence of the Five Factor Model. *Annual Review of Psychology* 40: 417–440.

Duncan, R. 1979. What Is the Right Organization Structure? Decision Tree Analysis Provides the answer. *Organizational Dynamics* 7 (Winter): 447–461.

Etzioni, A. 1964. *Modern Organizations*. Englewood Cliffs, NJ: Prentice Hall.

Evans, M. G. 1986. Organizational Behavior: The Central Role of Motivation. *Yearly Review of Management of the Journal of Management* 12: 203–222.

Feldman, D. C. 1976. A Practical Program for Employee Socialization. *Organizational Dynamics* 5: 64–80.

Feldman, D. C. 1981. The Multiple Socialization of Organization Members. *Academy of Management Review* 6: 309–318.

Fishbein, M., and I. Ajzen. 1975. Belief, Attitude, Intention and Behavior: An Introduction to Theory and Research. Reading, MA: Addison-Wesley.

Fisher, C. 1986. Organizational Socialization: An Integrative Review. In *Research in Personnel and Human Resource Management*, vol. 4. Edited by K. M. Rowland and G. R. Ferris. Greenwich, CT: JAI Press, 101–145.

Fisher, C. D., L. F. Schoenfeldt, and J. B. Shaw. 1995. *Human Resource Management*. Boston: Houghton Mifflin Company.

Flamholtz, E. G., and Y. Randle. 1998. *Changing the Game: Organizational Transformations of the First, Second, and Third Kinds*. New York: Oxford University Press.

Fox, J. 1998. Europe Is Heading for a Wild Ride. *Fortune* (August 17): 145–146, 148–149.

Fullerton, Jr., H. N. 1997. Labor Force 2006: Slowing Down and Changing Composition. *Monthly Labor Review* 120: 23–38.

Galbraith, J. R., and R. K. Kazanjian. 1986. *Strategy Implementation: Structure, Systems, and Process.* St. Paul, MN: West Publishing Company.

Garvin, D. A. 1988. *Managing Quality: The Strategic and Competitive Edge.* New York: Free Press.

Gehani, R. R. 1993. Quality Value–Chain: A Meta-Synthesis of Frontiers of Quality Movement. *Academy of Management Executive* 7: 29-42.

Glaser, R., and J. Kiecolt-Glaser. 1994. *Handbook of Human Stress and Immunity.* San Diego: Academic Press.

Goldhaber, G. M. 1993. *Organizational Communication.* Madison, WI: Brown & Benchmark.

Goldstone, R. L. 1998. Perceptual Learning. In *Annual Review of Psychology,* vol. 49. Edited by J. T. Spence, J. Darley, and D. J. Foss. Palo Alto: Annual Reviews, Inc., 585–612.

Goodstein, L. D., and W. W. Burke. 1991. Creating Successful Organizational Change. *Organizational Dynamics* 19 (Spring): 5–17.

Griener, L. E., and V. E. Schein. 1988. *Power and Organization Development.* Reading, MA: Addison-Wesley.

Griffin, R. W. 1982. *Task Design: An Integrative Approach.* Glenview, IL: Scott, Foresman.

Gross, N. and O. Port. 1998. The Next WAVE. *Business Week* (August 31): 80: 82–83.

Hackman, J. R., and G. Oldham. 1980. *Work Redeisgn.* Reading, MA: Addison-Wesley.

Hare, A. P. 1992. *Groups, Teams, and Social Interaction: Theories and Applications.* New York: Praeger.

Hayles, V. R., and A. M. Russell. 1997. *The Diversity Directive: Why Some Initiatives Fail & What to Do About It.* Chicago: Irwin Professional Publishing.

Herzberg, F. 1968. One More Time: How Do You Motivate Employees? *Harvard Business Review* (January–February): 53–62.

House, R. J., and M. L. Baetz. 1979. Leadership: Some Empirical Generalizations and New Research Directions. In *Research in Organizational Behavior,* ed. B. M. Staw. Greenwich, CT: JAI Press, 341–423.

House, R. J., and R. N. Aditya. 1997. The Social Scientific Study of Leadership: Quo Vadis? *Journal of Management* 23: 409–473.

Huber, G. P. 1980. *Managerial Decision Making.* Glenview, IL: Scott, Foresman and Company.

Information Week. 1993. A Cure for IBM's Blues? Retiring Exec Prescribes a Continuing Focus on Quality. *Information Week* (January 4): 48–49.

Jackson, S. E. and Associates, eds. 1992. *Diversity in the Workplace: Human Resources Initiatives.* New York: Guilford Press.

Jamieson, D., and J. O'Mara. 1991. *Managing Workforce 2000: Gaining the Diversity Advantage.* San Francisco: Jossey-Bass.

Johnston, W. B. 1991. Global Workforce 2000: The New Labor Market. *Harvard Business Review* 69: 115–129.

Kanfer, S. 1997. *Serious Business: The Art and Commerce of Animation in America from Betty Boop to Toy Story.* New York: Scribner.

Kanter, R. M. 1977. *Men and Women of the Corporation.* New York: Basic Books.

Kirkland, Jr., R. I. 1988. Entering a New Age of Boundless Competition. *Fortune* (March 14): 40–48.

Klein, N. M. 1993. *Seven Minutes: The Life and Death of the American Animated Cartoon.* New York: Verso.

Knapp, M. L., and J. A. Hall. 1997. *Nonverbal Communication in Human Interaction.* Fort Worth, TX: Harcourt Brace College Publishers.

Kroenke, D. M. 1992. *Management Information Systems.* New York: McGraw-Hill.

Lengnick-Hall, C. A. 1996. Customer Contributions to Quality: A Different View of the Customer-Oriented Firm. *Academy of Management Review* 21: 791–824.

Levine, J. M., and R. L. Moreland. 1990. Progress in Small Group Research. In *Annual Review of Psychology*, vol. 41. Edited by M. R. Rosensweig and L. W. Porter. Palo Alto, CA: Annual Reviews Inc., 585–634.

Lyles, M. A., and I. I. Mitroff. 1980. Organizational Problem Formulation: An Empirical Study. *Administrative Science Quarterly* 25: 102–119.

Madison, D. L., R. W. Allen, L. W. Porter, P. A. Renwick, and B. T. Mayes. 1980. Organizational Politics: An Exploration of Managers' Perceptions. *Human Relations* 33: 79–100.

Martin, J. 1992. *Cultures in Organizations: Three Perspectives.* New York: Oxford University Press.

Maslow, A. H. 1943. A Theory of Human Motivation. *Psychological Review* 50: 370–396.

Maslow, A. H., with D. C. Stephens and G. Heil. 1998. *Maslow on Management.* New York: John Wiley & Sons.

Mathis, R. and J. Jackson. 2000. *Human Resource Management.* Cincinnati: South-Western College Publishing.

Matteson, M. T., and J. M. Ivancevich. 1979. Organizational Stressors and Heart Disease: A Research Model. *Academy of Management Review* 4: 347–357.

Mayes, B. T., and R. W. Allen. 1977. Toward a Definition of Organizational Politics. *Academy of Management Journal* 2: 635–644.

McCrae, R. R., and P. T. Costa Jr. 1994. The Stability of Personality: Observations and Evaluations. *Current Directions in Psychological Science* 3: 173–175.

McGuire, W. J. 1985. Attitudes and Attitude Change. In *Handbook of Social Psychology*, vol II. Edited by G. Lindzey and E. Aronson. New York: Random House, 233–346.

Mintzberg, H. 1983. *Power In and Around Organizations.* Englewood Cliffs, NJ: Prentice Hall.

_____. 1987a. The Strategy Concept I: Five Ps for Strategy. *California Management Review* 30(1): 11–24.

_____. 1987b. The Strategy Concept II: Another Look at Why Organizations Need Strategies. *California Management Review* 30(1): 25–32

Mockler, R. J. 1984. *The Management Control Process.* Englewood Cliffs, NJ: Prentice Hall.

Mount, M. K., M. R. Barrick, and J. P. Strauss. 1994. Validity of Observer Ratings of the Big Five Personality Factors. *Journal of Applied Psychology* 72: 272–280.

Nadler, D. A., and M. L. Tushman. 1997. *Competing by Design: The Power of Organizational Architecture.* New York: Oxford University Press.

Nutt, P. C., and R. W. Backoff. 1997. Crafting Vision. *Journal of Management Inquiry* 6: 308–328.

Oldham, G. R. 1996. Job Design. Ch. 2 in *International Review of Industrial and Organizational Psychology.* Edited by C. L. Cooper and I. T. Robertson. Chichester, England: John Wiley & Sons, Ltd.

Ostry, S. 1990. Governments and Corporations in a Shrinking World: Trade and Innovation Policies in the United States, Europe, and Japan. *Columbia Journal of World Business* 25: 10–16.

Ott, J. S. 1989. *The Organizational Culture Perspective.* Pacific Grove, CA: Brooks/ Cole.

Pfeffer, J. 1992. *Managing with Power: Politics and Influence in Organizations.* Boston: Harvard Business School Press.

Pinder, C. C. 1998. Work Motivation in Organizational Behavior. Upper Saddle River, NJ: Prentice Hall.

Pinder, C. C. 1998. *Work Motivation in Organizational Behavior.* Upper Saddle River, NJ: Prentice Hall, Inc.

Pondy, L. R. 1967. Organizational Conflict: Concepts and Models. Administrative Science Quarterly 12: 296–320.

Porter, M. E. 1998. *On Competition.* Boston: Hazard Business Review Book Series.

Porter, L. W., and K. H. Roberts. 1976. Communication in Organizations. In *Handbook of Industrial and Organizational Psychology*, ed. M. D. Dunnette. Chicago: Rand McNally, Inc., 1567.

Pounds, W. E. The Process of Problem Finding. 1969. *Industrial Management Review* 11: 1–19.

Quain, J. R. 1998. How to Shop for a Palmtop. *Fast Company* (September): 196–203.

Quick, J. C., and J. D. Quick. 1984. *Organizational Stress and Preventive Management*. New York: McGraw-Hill.

Radford, G. S. 1922. *The Control of Quality in Manufacturing*. New York: Ronald Press.

Render, B., and J. Heizer. 1998. *Operations Management*. Englewood Cliffs, NJ: Prentice Hall.

Robbins, S. P. 1974. *Managing Organizational Conflict*. Englewood Cliffs, NJ: Prentice Hall.

Rubin, J. Z., D. G. Pruitt, and S. H. Kim. 1994. *Social Conflict: Escalation, Stalemate, and Settlement*. New York: McGraw-Hill.

Salancik, G. R., and J. Pfeffer. 1977. Who Gets Power and How They Hold Onto It: A Strategic Contingency Model of Power. *Organizational Dynamics* 5: 3–21.

Schein, E. H. 1968. Organizational Socialization and the Profession of Management. *Industrial Management Review* 9: 3.

Schein, E. H. 1984. Coming to a New Awareness of Organizational Culture. *Sloan Management Review* 25: 3–16.

Schein, E. H. 1992. *Organizational Culture and Leadership*. San Francisco: Jossey-Bass.

Scott, W. R. 1964. Theory of Organizations. In *Handbook of Modern Sociology*, ed. R. E. L. Faris. Chicago: Rand McNally, 485–529.

Selye, H. 1976. *The Stress of Life*. New York: McGraw-Hill.

Shannon, C. E., and W. Weaver. 1949. *The Mathematical Theory of Communication*. Urbana, IL: University of Illinois Press.

Sheppard, H. L., and N. Q. Herrick. 1972. *Where Have All the Robots Gone?* New York: Free Press.

Sheridan, W. 1972. *The Fall and Rise of Jimmy Hoffa*. New York: Saturday Review Press.

Snider, M., and W. Ickes. 1985. Personality and Social Behavior. In *Handbook of Social Psychology*, vol. 2. Edited by G. Lindzey and E. Aronson. New York: Random House, 883.

Stoner, J. A. F., and R. E. Freeman. 1992. *Management*. Englewood Cliffs, NJ: Prentice Hall.

Tjosvold, D. 1991. *The Conflict-Positive Organization: Stimulate Diversity and Create Unity*. Reading, MA: Addison-Wesley Longman.

Trice, H. M., and J. M. Beyer. 1993. *The Cultures of Work Organizations*. Englewood Cliffs, NJ: Prentice Hall.

Van Maanen, J., and E. H. Schein. 1977. Career Development. In *Improving Life at Work: Behavioral Science Approaches to Organizational Change*. Edited by J. R. Hackman and J. L. Suttle. Santa Monica: CA: Goodyear Publishing Company.

Van Maanen, J., and E. H. Schein. 1979. Toward a Theory of Organizational Socialization. In *Research in Organizational Behavior*, vol. 1. Edited by B. M. Staw and L. L. Cummings. Greenwich, CT: JAI Press, 209–264.

Walker, C. R., and R. Guest. 1952. *The Man on the Assembly Line* Cambridge, MA: Harvard University Press.

Weimer, B. 1992. *Human Motivation: Metaphors, Theories, and Research*. Newbury Park, CA: Sage Publications.

Wexley, K., and G. A. Yukl. 1977. *Organizational Behavior and Personnel Psychology*. Homewood, IL: Richard D. Irwin.

White, K. K. 1963. *Understanding the Company Organization Chart*. New York: American Management Association.

Wiggins, J. S., and A. L. Pincus. 1992. Personality: Structure and Assessment. *Annual Review of Psychology* 43: 473–504.

Wilson, C. Z., and M. Alexis. 1962. Basic Frameworks for Decisions. *Academy of Management Journal* 5: 150–164.

Wood, D. J. 1991. Corporate Social Performance Revisited. Academy of Management Review 16: 691–718.

Index